LYNN FRAZIER
WITH **GARRETT FRAZIER & DERRICK FRAZIER**

A WELL OF
WISDOM

THE PATH OF AN
UNCOMMON
MAN

RIVER GROVE
BOOKS

This book is a memoir reflecting the author's present recollections of experiences over time. Its story and its words are the author's alone. Some details and characteristics may be changed to protect the privacy of individuals, some events may be compressed, and some dialogue may be recreated.

Published by River Grove Books
Austin, TX
www.rivergrovebooks.com

Copyright ©2021 Lynn Frazier

All rights reserved.

Thank you for purchasing an authorized edition of this book and for complying with copyright law. No part of this book may be reproduced, stored in a retrieval system, or transmitted by any means, electronic, mechanical, photocopying, recording, or otherwise, without written permission from the copyright holder.
Cover Image: Texture of wood by monofaction,
used under license from Shutterstock.com
Portrait Photography by Megan Benavidez and Jason Page

Distributed by River Grove Books

Design and composition by Greenleaf Book Group
Cover design by Greenleaf Book Group

Publisher's Cataloging-in-Publication data is available.

Print ISBN: 978-1-63299-546-9

First Edition

To my family.
Thank you for all your patience and
the instrumental contributions.

To all the wonderful, hardworking, and talented people
who helped build Magnum into the huge worldwide success
we all enjoyed. Thank you for everything each and every
one of you contributed.

CONTENTS

Introduction	1
Chapter 1: Working the Land	7
Chapter 2: The Hands You Shake	27
Chapter 3: The Uncommon Man	43
Chapter 4: Follow the Oil	59
Chapter 5: Corpus Christi Calling	79
Chapter 6: The Ties That Bind	99
Chapter 7: Keepin' It Simple	119
Chapter 8: Mission Accomplished	133
Chapter 9: The Frazier Family Legacy	147
Chapter 10: Tapping Your Full Potential	163
Acknowledgments	177

─ INTRODUCTION

Everything was perfect.
The weather could not have been better. Eighty-five degrees, just a slight breeze. Calm seas surrounding the many islands of the Bahamas. Pristine water ideal for swimming, snorkeling, and fishing. Picture-postcard sunsets, which my sons, Garrett and Derrick, and I—our drinks and cigars in hand—would savor while sitting at the back of the 120-foot yacht reserved for our family. Fantastic, plentiful food, which we didn't have to worry about preparing, serving, or cleaning up. Exotic rums and other beverages, including those nonalcoholic umbrella drinks my nine-year-old granddaughter Olivia and eleven-year-old grandson Dylan sipped so proudly, always right at our fingertips.

We were in the expert hands of the seasoned crew of the *Mambo*, the boat we'd come to love so much that I thought about buying it. There was never any rush with our itinerary, just a peaceful blend of cruising, island-hopping, chasing the island pigs, feeding the sharks, spearfishing, and jet skiing.

Wi-Fi and cell phone service were spotty or nonexistent, but nobody was complaining. We weren't there for business. This was a time to let go of work, to totally de-stress. And, especially, it was a time to celebrate.

We had so much to celebrate on that June 2018 cruise. Right on top of the list was the love and closeness of our families. My oldest son, Garrett, and his wife, Trish, were on board with their kids, Olivia and her older brother Dylan. My son Derrick was enjoying rare couples' time with his wife, Ryan, who was pregnant with their third child, while their younger kiddos, Elliott and Wyatt, were back home with Ryan's parents. I was happy that my girlfriend, Anne, was able to join us.

Everyone was soaking up the endless moments to talk and laugh, or to just be with one another. Walking around the yacht in beach shorts and my favorite Hawaiian shirt, I would catch little glimpses of my family's enjoyment. One minute I might see Garrett guiding Olivia as she fearlessly jumped off the top of the boat into gin-clear water. The next minute I might spot Derrick quietly listening to Donald Sutherland narrating the audiobook version of *The Old Man and the Sea* by Ernest Hemingway.

But we had something else to celebrate on this five-day cruise that my "boys" had organized and that I was happy to be paying for. That "something else" helped to make this trip the beautiful experience that none of us will ever forget. When we boarded that private yacht in the Bahamas, we were on the home stretch of strategizing the sale of our family company, Magnum Oil Tools International. The results of the final transaction would put one big stamp on our astounding success, while opening a wide door to our future. When the ink was dry and the deal was made public a few months later, Magnum had been sold to Nine Energy Service for nearly half a billion dollars!

So, when my two sons and I would sit at the back of the *Mambo* at sunset, we were doing more than just puffing our cigars and sipping our aged dark rum. We were basking in the reality that we were about to cash in on our life's work. We could feel secure that as we explored our new horizons, individually and together, we would never have to worry about the financial part of the picture.

I don't remember everything that the three of us said or did as the days and evenings gently rolled by. I remember toasts to our success, and I know there were hugs—real hugs, not those shoulder bumps that men usually settle for. We didn't need words to communicate what we were feeling, what this Bahamas getaway was really all about. I suppose that if somebody was filming those moments for some Netflix movie, you might hear one or another of us say something like this:

"We did it!"

"The prize is in sight!"

"We waited and waited for this moment, and here it is!"

Yes, we had made it. We had fulfilled a mission that began all the way back in 1985, when I had a dream that I could make something big happen with my own business, providing tools and services to oil and gas companies all over the world. I found the nerve to chase after that dream and to keep following the long and challenging journey to the finish line. I navigated the first leg of that journey before the boys were old enough to join me, and for the second leg I was fortunate enough to have them both by my side. So much happened on that journey, so many events and experiences that shaped my life and the lives of those I loved. . . .

Today, a couple of years after that celebration cruise in the Bahamas, I'm taking time out from my new personal and professional ventures to embark on a different kind of mission. I want to tell the story of how I've lived and what I've learned so far. I'll turn the clock back, not just to the 1985 founding of Magnum but much further back. I will bring in many of the people and places that helped to shape me, guide me, inspire me, and show me something important and meaningful as I found my way. In this book, I'm going to open up my memory bank and shine a little light on what I've done and how I've done it.

I have to admit it never seems right when I say what *I've* done. I could never have achieved this success without tons of help and support from so many others who have traveled parts of this journey with me. At so many points along the way, I probably could not have moved even one inch forward without their endless and generous contributions. I also know that I could never have gotten where I've come to without making more than my share of mistakes. I'll try to be as honest as I can be in talking about those missteps and the lessons I gained from them.

I'll also point out some of my ideas about what it takes to succeed in business and in life. When I think about some of my core beliefs, here's one that jumps to the top of the list: To achieve the full potential meant for us in our lives, we need to aspire for something higher, something more. And we have to keep aspiring, keep dreaming, keep striving for what really matters to us, what fills us with life.

Even on that perfect Bahamas cruise in 2018, I found myself reminding Garrett and Derrick that we've got to keep aspiring to something new, something more. We can't just sit back passively because we earned the opportunity to do so. We've got to keep our sights focused on where we're going next and how we're going to get there.

Because so much of my story includes Garrett and Derrick, I'll be talking a lot about them in the chapters ahead. This book is my story, but it's also the Frazier family story too. And because I'm not a guy who likes to stand alone in the spotlight, I will sometimes hand the microphone over to my sons and invite them to speak directly about their own experiences on this family adventure. I'm looking forward to hearing what they have to say, and I bet there'll be a few surprises!

This book is meant as a gift, first and foremost, to all those in our extended Frazier family. It's a time capsule to capture this whole Magnum ride, and who and what has been driving it. My hope is that you will find something that will encourage you to dream, to aspire, to believe you can go out there and make things happen for yourself and for those you love.

Introduction

My wish is that you begin to recognize your own potential and take the steps every day to achieve it.

I also extend this same hope to others outside our family and circle of loved ones who may have picked up this book. Whether you're a man or a woman, whether you are young or not so young, may you discover something while reading my little book that encourages or inspires you to believe that you may someday achieve and celebrate your own kind of success.

It's time to get started. I'm new at all this, so the only way I know how to begin is to take you back to the time and place where I grew up. We're going to set our GPS for a few stops in the rural heartland of South Texas, back in the 1950s and '60s. You'll get to visit a time and place where a young boy learned to work hard, to do what he was told, and, oh, maybe have an adventure or two!

CHAPTER 1

Working the Land

Let me begin my story by taking you inside one of my earliest childhood memories:

I'm five years old, and I'm sitting on a tractor in one of the tin sheds on my grandpa's farm in Calhoun County, Texas. As I raise my small hands and grip the wheel, I look out from my perch on the seat of that tractor on this typically hot South Texas morning, imagining the day when I can drive up and down the fields of my grandparents' farm. Tilling the soil. Pulling the trailer full of hay bales. Feeding the cows. Completing each and every task and chore that needs to be done, as the sun slowly dips in the wide-open blue sky above. Closing my eyes to soak up that image, I feel like I've died and gone to heaven....

Farming is very much in my blood, and life on and around the farm provided many of my most important lessons about work and life. Soon after I was born as the oldest of four children and the eldest grandchild, we lived next to my grandparents' home in a two bedroom house. Inside our large family circle, this little house on the Whatley farm was known as the "Weaning House." It took its name from its role as the place young couples moved into right after they got married, before they could afford a home of their own. My mom and dad were the first to use it in this capacity.

That Weaning House is gone now, but the home my grandparents lived in for many years still stands, right there on Whatley Road, which was named for my grandparents' family. That farm had a couple of hundred acres back then, but in the world of farming in Texas, we would be considered one of the little guys.

Farming goes way back in my mother's family, the Whatleys. My great-grandparents had been farmers in Ireland before they immigrated to the United States in the 1800s to escape the potato famine. After first settling in Alabama, the family eventually moved to Texas. My grandfather was born and raised in Fort Worth, but as a young man he worked at a cotton gin in Austwell, a small community not far from the area where I was raised. He bought his first 160-acre farm close to Austwell in a community called Green Lake soon after the Great Depression of the 1930s, and he just kept going from there.

Having family around was something I always enjoyed. I have very fond memories of visiting my uncle Anthony and aunt Dorothy in Tivoli when I was a boy. A bunch of us kids in the family would take off as soon as we arrived early in the morning, and the grown-ups wouldn't see us again until dark. We liked to explore the area around "Pee Creek," so named because the septic system from a few of the surrounding homes ran into it. Surprisingly, the creek didn't smell all that bad. We knew better than to actually go splashing around in the water,

though. We just enjoyed playing on the hillside along the banks of the creek. In the flat lands of Texas, any hill or ditch was always an attraction.

My mom met my dad, Lester Edwin Frazier, in Port Lavaca when they were teenagers. I didn't hear the story of how they got to know each other until I was much older. My dad was born in Colorado, but his parents divorced when he was ten or eleven, and his father moved to Utah. During my dad's youth, he lived with his brother for a while. During his stays, he would work in uranium mines nearby driving trucks; but when he was a teenager, he would come down to Port Lavaca in the winter with his mother and his stepfather, Charlie, who sought to escape the cold and snow of Colorado. Since Charlie earned his living as a barber, he was able to find temporary work in Texas.

My father took a risk and bought the local Phillips 66 service station located along Main Street in Port Lavaca, with its population of about 10,000. When Lynda Whatley drove up to that Phillips 66, Lester Frazier apparently took a shine to her.

Well, things have a way of coming full circle in Texas. After my parents moved out of the Weaning House, my father went back to work at that same Phillips 66 station. We lived in Port Lavaca then, and what I remember most about our house was the huge front porch. When I took my kids back to see that house many years later, I discovered that this "huge" porch was no more than twelve feet long and ten feet wide. Strange how we remember things from our childhood as being much bigger than they are.

When they put in the bypass that skirted downtown Port Lavaca, business at the Phillips 66 station dried up. After this, my dad landed a job operating heavy equipment as his primary job for a construction company. Once again, after another transition from that job, we found ourselves back on the farm. This time, instead of working the land on the Whatley farm, we lived and worked on the adjacent Clark farm.

That's where I really began to learn what it meant to work hard every day. Any time that I was not at school or doing my homework, my dad would send me out into the fields to work with the Hispanic migrant farmhands that he hired. The "Hands" as we called them, lived in houses my family had built for them on the farm and got paid by my father in cash. At one point, long before I was as old as any of those farmhands, my dad even had me directing those guys out there on their tractors working our cotton and other crops. I learned to communicate pretty well in Spanish.

Working the Land

As my mother often said, "When you live on the farm, everybody works." My younger siblings—my brother Lloyd, my sister Michelle, and my brother Lorne—all played their part as they got older. When I was only nine, my dad taught me to drive the tractor out in the fields. He'd drop me off at first light with my lunch packed, and he'd pick me up at dusk. He even taught me how to drive the farm pickup truck around that time, moving the seat all the way up to the steering wheel just so I could reach the pedal and see out the windshield.

Mom would be right out there in the fields working alongside us, often driving a tractor or grain truck. She likes to tell the story of the night she nearly ran right smack into a black panther. Sometimes Mom would get back to the house late, but she always made time to cook for us. It wasn't uncommon for us to sit down to a dinner of pancakes.

Most of the time, though, we ate very well because Mom was a great cook. Since we had our own chickens, we always had plenty of eggs. We also butchered some of the cattle, sheep, and pigs that we raised, and we hunted deer, wild hogs, quail, and dove. With a winter garden and a summer garden, we had a wide assortment of fresh vegetables and fruit. Our garden would provide us with squash, beets, okra, green beans, cantaloupe, and watermelon; we also enjoyed dewberries, peaches, and oranges from our fruit trees. Some of my favorite meals were fried chicken, venison, and meat loaf.

My dad was very resourceful, always on the lookout for new ways to earn money to feed our family. At one point he raised a couple of thousand rabbits. People would drive south from Houston to purchase these rabbits. Later he would begin to travel to a market twenty-five miles up the road to Victoria, the nearest "big city" from Port Lavaca. I remember toting fifty-pound bags of feed on the feed cart, slowing down at each cage, which had a tray to feed the rabbits.

Much later, after I had gone off to college, my dad began buying and breeding exotic birds. He constructed and organized dozens of bird cages throughout the thick trees behind my parents' house for all his toucans, macaws, parrots, cockatoos, and yellow-naped amazons, just to name a few. The neighbors would say that they always knew by the screeching when it was feeding time for those birds. When he was just starting out with this venture, my dad ran an ad in the local newspaper inquiring whether anyone was looking for a new home for their pet birds. Believe it or not, some people would just give away their exotic birds, or sell them at a very cheap price. Sometimes my dad might turn around and sell those birds for a nice profit, finding that home they were looking for.

We didn't continue to work the land on the Clark farm for my entire childhood. At some point we moved into a house that was built in the early 1900s on the Victoria Barge Canal, where my dad plunged into the cattle business as well. We would remain there until I graduated from high school.

That place was near the upper banks on the barge canal with a view of Green Lake, which at two miles wide and thirteen miles in circumference holds the distinction of being the largest natural freshwater lake in the whole state of Texas. The lake got its name from its greenish waters, but make no mistake: This was not some beautiful body of water that people loved to wade and swim in. It was more of a swamp, far more agreeable to the snakes, turtles, and gators that heavily populated it. As my father would say, "You can walk across Green Lake." The area near our ranch had more than its share of alligators, which we didn't hunt, although we did hunt the wild hogs.

This was the kind of place that held many mysterious stories about the past. A guy who worked for us would tell of the story of the day the horse he was riding came up lame and stopped to rest on a tree trunk. Upon closer inspection, that tree trunk turned out to be a cannon. As the legend goes, the cannon had been placed there by a pirate who had come up the Guadalupe River with a treasure that he desperately needed to hide. Apparently, that pirate never lived to come back and retrieve his treasure. You can bet that every effort was made by the folks living around there to locate and dig up that treasure. To this day, nobody has found it.

People in South Texas love to tell stories, and they don't hold back just because you don't happen to be family or friends. As they would say where I grew up, "People will talk half an hour to a wrong number."

My dad liked to get out among folks to shoot the breeze when he had the chance. He had a couple of favorite beer joints with pool tables where several of the farmers hung out, and sometimes, when I was a little boy, he had me tag along with him. Now when your dad is drinking his fill at a beer joint, you've got to learn to occupy yourself. I would just sit on the floor playing with the pool balls or looking for other things to bide my time. Of course, my dad didn't let me drink *my* first beer until I was getting ready to leave for college. That summer he bought me my first beer at the Do Drop Inn beer joint in our hometown of Port Lavaca.

Looking back on my upbringing, I can see how my father's willingness to change directions and follow new paths to earn a living left a major imprint on me. Many years later, I would come to understand that to fully open the gate to major success, you need to avoid getting stuck trying to follow one straight and narrow path. You've got to stay ready to follow all those zigs and zags that will keep showing up along your trail.

My dad's work ethic also left a big impression on me. From the very beginning, I understood that if you want to fulfill any mission in life, you've got to be willing to toil and sweat long hours every day. But if I had to name my dad's most important influence on me, it would have to be a sense of discipline.

You walked the chalk line with my dad. If you were five minutes late coming home from school, getting back from a date, or showing up in  the fields to work the farm, you were grounded. No excuses, no discussion. He used the belt when he believed it was needed to teach you a lesson, and yes, I got the belt my share of times. He would lean me over my bed and deliver my punishment after he caught me picking on my brother Lloyd, who was four years younger than me, or when I didn't do something I had been told to do.

I loved football and began playing on the seventh-grade team. I remember the day during the following season when my eighth-grade football coach pulled me aside while I was getting dressed for practice. "Lynn," he said, "what the hell happened to you?" I probably made up some story to cover the truth, but with the bruises and welt lines running from my waist down to the backs of my knees, I wasn't fooling anybody.

I wouldn't say that getting the belt made me angry at my dad. Mostly, it just made me afraid. And that fear kept me in line, ensuring that I would do whatever needed to be done each and every time, so as to never get the belt again. No excuses.

Working the Land

My dad called upon some other ways to teach me a tough lesson. When I was three, I sucked my thumb. Now, that may not sound unusual for a kid that age, but to my dad it was something that a boy just shouldn't be doing if he was going to grow up to be a man. At first, he stood back and let my mom try to solve the problem. Her first strategy was to put pepper on my thumb. Well, that pepper may have made me sneeze a bunch of times, but it didn't slow down my thumb-sucking. Next, she tried wrapping my thumb in tape. Even if that tape didn't taste so good, I kept sucking my thumb.

That's when my dad decided that he had watched and waited long enough—he would take matters into his own hands.

"Lynn, get out of bed!" he commanded as he stormed into my room early one morning. "Go to your closet and take out your suitcase. Put in some shirts, some socks, and some underwear. When you're done, come on out to the car."

When he saw me moving a bit too slowly for his purposes, he said, "Let's go! Let's get your suitcase in the trunk." Noticing my confused and frightened look, he explained, "You're going to live with the 'Hands.'"

"Why, Dad?" I muttered as I tried to hold off the tears. "Why do I have to go away?"

"Because you won't quit sucking your thumb!"

By then my mom had stepped outside. With just one look, she knew exactly what was happening.

"Now, Lester," she said in a firm tone.

"Well," he said, looking me dead in the eye, "if we let you stay home, are you going to quit sucking your thumb?"

"I will, Daddy; I'll quit," I mumbled through my shivering body and streaming tears.

I never sucked my thumb again.

A few years later, my dad decided he had to teach me another lesson. At that time, my dad smoked a couple of packs of cigarettes a day, and I knew that he kept his cartons of cigarettes up on top of our refrigerator. One day, while I was working out in the fields, a farmhand motioned for me to come over to him.

"Hey, amigo," Lupito said to me, "you got any cigarettes?" I was no more than seven or eight years old at the time. Wanting to show him I was a really big boy, I replied, "Well, not on me, but I know where my dad keeps them." Looking each way to make sure my dad wasn't around, I slipped inside the house and grabbed a pack of cigarettes from on top of the fridge. After I hustled outside and handed it to Lupito, he immediately opened the pack and lit up a cigarette. He took a few puffs and then held his cigarette out toward me. Again, wanting to look older and more mature, I accepted the offer. After coughing my way through a couple of drags, I handed the cigarette back to Lupito, with my best grown-up nod of thanks. Yes, I was proud to have taken this step toward adulthood, but otherwise I didn't think much more about my little clandestine act. Until dinner time.

"Lynn, come over here a minute," my dad said as he approached the dinner table. "I am missing a pack of cigarettes," he went on, pointing to the top of the refrigerator. "Did you take one?"

Working the Land

I knew that my dad could always detect when something like a pack of cigarettes was missing, so there was no point in making up a story.

"Yes, sir," I said.

"And did you smoke any of those cigarettes?"

"No, sir, I gave 'em to Lupito."

When my dad simply nodded, I thought maybe he was just proud of me being all grown up. So, after we finished dinner, I didn't suspect anything when he motioned for me to go off with him to the Green Lake Stop & Shop to pick up some milk and a few other groceries Mom needed. At the store, I was too busy checking out the candy aisle to notice everything he plopped into the cart, so it was a surprise when we got home and he pulled out a huge green cigar. And an even bigger surprise when he held that big ol' cigar out to me and said, "Sit down over here."

I immediately did what I was told. "Now, I want you to smoke this cigar. Smoke it all the way down to the nub." He lit it for me and told me to puff on it. He and Mom were about to go outside to talk. He turned before walking out the front door. "Smoke it all," he commanded. "You hear me?"

I knew that he would be tracking my progress. No way could I back down. Before that big green cigar was half smoked, I thought I was going to vomit. A few puffs later, I thought I was going to die. But I did what I was told, finishing that cigar down to the nub.

A little while later, my dad and mom came back into the house. He opened the back door, and she opened the front door at the other end so they could get all the thick and heavy cigar smoke out.

"Now," my father said as he noticed me still coughing from my cigar intake, "I don't want you to ever smoke anything again. Is that understood?"

I nodded between coughs. And I never smoked again.

I'll give my father credit. By the time I left for college, he had actually quit smoking himself.

My dad remained strict even through my teenage years, but I knew that he really did love me. His influence on my life had begun very early, beginning with my name: Warren Lynn. I was named Warren after my grandfather and Lynn after dad's childhood best friend, from what I was told. After visiting Colorado with my dad's childhood friend, Lynn, my dad decided that I should be called Lynn. That name has stuck with me right up to today.

There's no question that my dad succeeded in instilling a strong sense of discipline in me. I learned that when there was something to be done, you just plunged right in and did it. You didn't hesitate, and you didn't stop until it was done . . . and done right.

He also taught me that if you tried to step out of line and stray from the right course of action, you would eventually suffer the consequences. That was another important lesson that I would carry with me throughout my business career.

I have no regrets about my dad's way of teaching me these hard lessons. And I will always remember him as the great man he was. He passed away well into my adulthood, in September 2013.

When it came to church, my mom was a regular attendee at our little Baptist church, and she made sure we came with her. She taught Bible classes, and I would hold the altar plates during Sunday services. But my dad? He would show up on Christmas and Easter—maybe. He would insist that he was not worried one bit about winding up in hell, though. As he would say, "I'll be so busy shaking hands, it won't make no difference where I am."

Our family was big enough to provide me with other sources of learning. Uncle Charles was a major influence on me. We were only about ten years apart, so he was almost like a buddy. We always played and did stuff around the farm. I also picked up many useful lessons from Uncle Anthony and Uncle Ricky, who had a different connection to farming. They were crop dusters, and they became very successful at their profession. Every rice and cotton farmer in Calhoun County had to apply chemicals to their crops, either by tractor or by plane, and using crop dusters was obviously a much quicker and more efficient way to go. And since my uncles had little or no crop-dusting competition, they tended to be the go-to crop dusters for just about every farm in our area of South Texas.

When I got to be thirteen or fourteen, my uncles began taking me under their wing, so to speak. Uncle Anthony and Uncle Ricky would put in very long days, flying from daylight to dusk every day for all but a couple of months of the year. When I showed an interest in what they were doing, they taught me how to help. Sometimes I would be in the hanger mixing the poisons for them, and just before they took off, I would connect the hose and fill their planes with the needed contents for their flights. With the rice farms, they used big trucks filled with a granular fertilizer to load the plane. When the plane would pull up to the truck, I would be the one to dump that fertilizer inside their planes.

My uncles both became excellent businessmen. In addition to the money he made from crop dusting, Uncle Anthony inherited some land from one of his uncles. Apparently, that land happened to have some valuable mineral rights to oil and gas on it. On many occasions I would listen to Uncle Anthony talk to the other guys he knew about what he could do with that land. Sometimes he would bring me into the discussions. I was impressed by the way he would consider various options, never feeling tied down to one narrow perspective in his approach to money and business. In a way, he was already helping to give me a road map for how I would navigate my own business decisions many years later.

Uncle Anthony taught me another valuable lesson. As well as he did with his crop-dusting business and his property investments—and you would be amazed if I told you just how high he soared on his financial flight path—he and Aunt Dorothy to this day live in the same modest house they've owned for decades. That taught me that you don't have to become flashy when you begin to do well in business. Instead of throwing money around on fancy cars, big houses, and other big-ticket purchases, you could choose to save and invest your money wisely. As the years rolled by, that would leave you in a much stronger financial state.

As pilots of small planes with a nephew who was curious about what they did and how they did it, my uncle Warren, who also was a crop duster, decided that I ought to be doing more than just loading their planes. He was determined to get me up there in the air with him.

On some of our close-to-home flights, we did a little outlaw hunting, tracking deer in the ranch next to ours. When we got close enough to shoot, Uncle Warren would use both hands to grip his rifle and pull the trigger, leaving me to do my best to hold the stick on the plane. Since we didn't crash, I guess I did well enough.

When we touched ground and approached our kill, Uncle Warren tied up the deer's antlers and told me it was too heavy to put in the back of the plane. I would have to lie out on the opposite wing strut for balance. The deer would have to be placed underneath and tied to the wing strut, with me out there making sure we could fly. It wasn't until long after we had gotten home and gutted that deer that I thought about how crazy that was. Not wanting my parents to find out all the details of my little flying adventure, Uncle Warren swore me to secrecy.

I was getting more and more fascinated with flying. It seemed like these little planes could fly anywhere, even under bridges or electric highline wires. At one time, the house we were living in had a thirty-foot TV antenna on the roof. It wasn't unusual for either of my uncles to fly by and buzz our house, often coming within what seemed like inches of that antenna. In fact, there was a day when one of my uncles flew so close he had to pull up fast at the last second to miss clipping it.

Apparently, that maneuver put a drain on the Piper Cub's fuel. A minute later, I heard that frightening "buzz, buzz, buzz" sound as the plane sputtered and dipped. My fear was rising by the second as I watched him make an abrupt, shaky landing on the field right beside our house. That put the clamps on my enthusiasm about flying for a while.

Closer to home, my mom gave me good grades for how well I watched over my younger siblings. Well, mostly good grades anyway. She was also extra proud of me when I caught a calf at a rodeo in Houston and got to bring him home to raise him on our ranch. Another time, she marveled at how I managed to ride a horse and not fall off an icy cliff in Colorado one winter when I had gone up to help members of my dad's family drive cattle from higher elevations down to a valley.

I also got pretty good at hunting ducks, deer, and wild hogs. When I was out having fun with my friends, you didn't have to dare me to jump off the pilings of the Victoria Barge Canal Bridge. One summer my dad bought 150 crab traps, which I put out into Green Lake to catch crabs. I caught enough to sell to the nearby shrimp houses and to employees at Union Carbide and the nearby plastics plant. I believe I made a good bit of money for college selling crabs that summer.

My mom would say that I was a kid who liked to get myself right in the middle of everything, and she was always there to pick me up whenever I stumbled during one of my many adventures. Everyone in our family remembers that Halloween night of the scavenger hunt in the local cemetery. The cemetery thick with tombstones was scary stuff for the young kids, and I decided that I would add a little something extra to their fright. My best friend Kim Evans and I each tied a bedsheet around our necks and rode toward that cemetery on our motorcycles. I had a tape recorder prepared to scare everyone with recordings of shrieks and screams as they ran away from these terrifying ghosts on wheels.

The only problem was that my sheet got caught in the sprocket of the rear wheel of my motorcycle as I was driving fifty miles per hour on the highway on the way to the cemetery. With the sheet caught up in the wheel, my face was jerked to the right, plunging it right into the wheel. The motorcycle and I crashed. With the motorcycle on top of me, I was sliding down the middle of the road. After coming to a stop, I lay there choking and bleeding, with my right leg stuck up against the hot muffler. I'm telling you, that leg was sizzling like bacon! Kim got the motorcycle off me and left to get help, while I remained in the middle of the road wondering what had just happened. Eventually, in an effort to get to safety, we were able to put the motorcycle in the back of Kim's pickup truck. I was bleeding so much out of my eye that I couldn't see where we were going. While backing up to turn around, Kim reversed into the ditch, getting us stuck. Well, I had to get out to help push the truck out of the ditch. We got back to the house, and I couldn't wait to look in the mirror to see what had happened to my face because I couldn't see. That's when I found out that my eyelid was cut wide open and in half, although I could still see my bloody footprints on my way back to the car.

So, as it turned out, the only "kid" who really got scared in this whole escapade was me. My mom finally got me to the hospital for stitches, and since this was far from my first mishap that left me in need of getting sewed up, the doctor turned to my mom and said, "Lynda, you should learn how to put in the stitches yourself. You'd save a whole lot of time and money."

Working the Land

At Calhoun High School, where I was a standout linebacker for the Sandcrabs' football team, they started calling me "the Ghost Rider" after this incident. The most embarrassing part about this adventure was that it reminded everybody that of all the kids around our family and our neighborhood, I was the one who would scare the easiest. My family loved to tell the story about that night we watched *The Exorcist* in the Port Lavaca movie house. After we drove home, I ran out of my car as soon as I rolled into our driveway. When my brother jumped on my back as I walked in the front door, I screamed so loud I probably woke up the nearest neighbor four miles away. I still haven't lived that one down.

After my Ghost Rider episode, I don't think I was much for motorcycle riding. But, a year later, my brother, sister, and I were dropped off by the school bus at the end of the half-mile road to the house. We were all getting into the car when I saw a rattlesnake crawling under the car. Nothing new about that when you live in rural South Texas, but this snake was headed right for my brother and sister on the other side of the car. After I grabbed it by the tail and pulled it from under the car out in the open, it coiled up. I tossed my brother the keys to the trunk to get the tire iron out. But even after I pinned that snake's head down and cut its head half off with the sharp end of the tire iron, it still managed to pull its head out from under my foot and bite me through my tennis shoe on my big toe with one fang.

"Get in the car," Mom said, shaking her head as she drove me off to the hospital. Then she added, "Take your shoelace out of your tennis shoe and tie it around your ankle."

At the hospital, in addition to giving me twenty-one anti-venom shots, they had to cut into the bite and let it bleed out. My family left the room to go fill out paperwork. Sitting there alone with my fear and frustration, I called out to them, "I'm bleeding to death in here!" Before the doc finished up with me, he nodded to my mom and said, "Like I told you, Lynda, you got to learn how to put those stitches in yourself."

This adventure gave me a new name on the football team and around school: "The Rattlesnake Kid."

Kids everywhere have their own growing-up adventures, I suppose, but mine somehow seemed bigger than life at the time and in the retelling of the stories years later. I was able to record the details of many of these experiences by writing everything down in my school year record books, which would include not only the names of my teachers and subjects I took but also my new friends and things that happened to me each year. I still have all those school record books.

My mom is a walking treasure chest of stories about all of her kids and everybody else who has been part of her family. Her living room is like a museum, its walls capturing so many of the individuals and places important in our family history. To honor the memory of her grandfather, who once rode a horse as a guard on a prison farm, she displays his shotgun, badge, and spurs.

When my mom was recently asked to look back on all my exploits and adventures and comment on what they might reveal about me and my childhood influences, she said something that really stuck with me: "Lynn could always figure out whatever he had to do to deal with any situation he found himself in."

When you stop and think about that for a moment, you've got to admit that those are pretty good words to describe the makings of a successful business owner.

CHAPTER 2

THE HANDS YOU SHAKE

I have always believed that we learn many of our most important lessons during some of our toughest times. That was definitely true for me as it relates to something that happened during my second semester of college.

Back in high school, I was never much better than a high-C, low-B student. So, it wasn't surprising that I ran into my share of challenges after enrolling at Texas A&I University in Kingsville (now Texas A&M University-Kingsville), where I played football.

Chemistry stood out as the biggest obstacle for me and many of my classmates. The word around campus was that everybody struggled with the chemistry course taught by Dr. Beran, a highly respected professor known for his very difficult classes. My roommate and I, and another guy across the hall in our dorm, were all taking Dr. Beran's class together. For the first few weeks, we kept our heads above water. Then came the first test.

When we got those tests handed back to us, you could add all three of our scores together and you wouldn't get much over 100. The guy who lived across the hall from me did so poorly he dropped the class. However, my roommate and I decided to stick with it and give it our all. As the semester ended, we received our final grades. My roommate wound up with a sixty-two, and I got a fifty-eight. I had failed the class.

Knowing I had to act, I went right up to Dr. Beran after everybody else had cleared the classroom. I was hoping to talk him up a couple of points on my grade, although of course that's not what I told him.

"I've never failed anything in my life," I blurted out. "Can you tell me what I could have done better?"

Dr. Beran listened patiently for a moment, but from his stern facial expression I could tell that he was not going to be changing my grade. When he finally spoke, he didn't start lecturing me about my study habits. He didn't question my motivation. He didn't even ask me how many nights I was spending driving up Highway 44 to party in the big city of Corpus Christi. Instead, he just leaned over to pat me on the shoulder.

"Young man, I'm going to tell you something, and I want you to remember this for the rest of your life," Dr. Beran began. "You really have to focus to do well in life. But even more important than that, remember this, son: It's not the grades you make; it's the hands you shake."

Then he gathered all his papers, stacked them neatly in his briefcase, and walked out of the empty classroom. At first, I couldn't wrap my mind around what my chemistry professor was trying to tell me. It sure didn't seem to have much to do with improving my grade on that chemistry test and passing the course. I lowered my head and walked out of the class. Then, a little later in life, I got it: If I was serious about getting a "passing grade" or achieving success in my personal and professional life, what really mattered would be my willingness and my ability to meet people, talk to people, listen to people, get to know people, and make them aware of my interests and my burning desire to work hard and get ahead. No one ever asked me for my GPA.

Shaking as many hands as I could meant making myself known to all kinds of people I would come across, no matter how "important" they may at first appear to be. You never know who might be the person who could open a door that changes your life.

Over time, I came to see that Dr. Beran's advice would have another important meaning for me. The number of hands I would shake also could apply to being an up-front and personable business owner, someone who would devote a whole lot of time and attention to meeting, spending time with, and really getting to know the people who worked for him. It meant being a leader who genuinely cared about his people, tuning in not only to what they did in their job roles but also to who they were, and what they needed from me to feel supported and valued.

I can't say I had all these big meanings of Dr. Beran's words figured out two minutes after I walked out of chemistry class that day. But I definitely filed his message away. It wouldn't be long until I experienced a major example of how it would serve me.

Before I get to that part of my story, though, I've got to tell you about another man in another situation where I learned invaluable lessons during my college days. We're going to take a time-out to talk some football, Texas football! I want to share with you how I even came to be playing college football and just how important that experience was in shaping me.

As I mentioned earlier, I was a pretty decent football player at Calhoun High School in Port Lavaca. I played linebacker primarily, but at six feet and 185 pounds, I was not exactly huge for the position. Still, I carried a deep-seated belief that I could make it as a college football player. Without venturing far from home, I hustled my way to an invitation to try out with the Texas A&I University Javelinas as a walk-on. I made the team, a significant accomplishment in itself. But I had higher goals. Because my parents could not really afford to pay for college, my sights were set on earning a full athletic scholarship.

Most of the other defensive players at Texas A&I were a lot bigger and stronger than me, and many of those guys had made all-state teams at much larger schools than Calhoun High. Some of them would even go on to play pro football. But I just stepped out on that field unafraid, like I belonged. I busted my butt and soon earned that scholarship. Lifting the burden of paying for my college education was a huge relief.

Being awarded that scholarship was not the only benefit I gained from being part of the Texas A&I Javelinas football program. Playing for Coach Gil Steinke helped to build a foundation that I would call upon throughout my professional career and my life.

Now, some of you non-Texans may be wondering, what exactly is a javelina anyway? The short answer is that a javelina, more formally known as a peccary, is an animal that looks a lot like a pig except for its small ears and its tail that's not easily seen from a distance. Javelinas, which can grow to more than eighty pounds and pack a mean punch with their warthog-like tusks, are common in many areas of Texas, as well as Arizona, New Mexico, and parts of South America.

Back then, the Javelinas of Texas A&I University were simply winners. Yep, we were a true football powerhouse. In fact, during my two seasons on the team, in 1974 and '75, we were Lone Star Conference champions, and we went on to win two NAIA national championships. We dominated the competition so thoroughly that we triumphed in those national championship games by the score of 34–23 over the Henderson State Reddies in '74 and 37–0 over the Salem Spirits in '75.

One of the best parts about playing on such a powerhouse is that during all our blowout victories, the starters would get rested early. For second stringers like myself, that meant that instead of sitting and watching all day from the bench, we got to be out there on the field for as long or longer than the first stringers.

Head Coach Gil Steinke had played for Texas A&I University himself and had even gone on to make it in the NFL with the Philadelphia Eagles. He came back to coach at his alma mater and had been highly successful in guiding the football program for twenty years by the time I came along.

This was a guy who really knew his football. He also knew how to build a team, how to communicate with all kinds of players, and how to lead. Under Coach Steinke's leadership, we always had great team spirit. We just carried ourselves as a tight, cohesive unit. Yes, sir, we had each other's backs, no matter what.

I remember one game where we had to dig deep to call upon those close bonds. It was a day when we faced a rare challenge from an opponent. I'm not sure about all the details, but the best I can recall is that we were playing Abilene Christian and, with about seven minutes left in that game, we found ourselves behind by a score of 27–0. That was unknown territory for our team. We huddled on the sidelines, and the message from Coach Steinke was simple:

"Guys, we're better than this. Let's figure out what's going on right now. No finger-pointing, just a gut check of what we're not doing as a team. It's time to come together and play as one. Let's play the way we know how to play!"

Coach Steinke diagrammed a trick play, which immediately led to our first touchdown. We kicked an onside kick and recovered it, leading to a second touchdown. Then we made a couple of defensive stops and scored twice again, tying the game 27–27. We just were not going to be beaten! We would have won that game if it had lasted a few more seconds because the final whistle blew just as we had driven to within range of our ace field goal kicker.

Everybody on our team loved playing for Coach Steinke, and we always wanted to give him more than 100 percent effort. He just had a way about him. He wasn't one of those coaches who would be jumping all over you and hollering at you for every little mistake. He would just sit you down, calmly look you in the eye, and explain to you what you needed to do to get better. You knew that he cared about you, that he valued you, that he believed in you.

Many years later, when I was seeking to achieve the highest possible levels of success with my own business, I would remember the example of Coach Steinke when I sat down to talk to my employees as individuals or as a team. I understood that if I really wanted to get the best from them, I would need to show them that I cared about them, valued them, and believed in them. I would do my best to avoid jumping on them or hollering at them, and I would show them that I always had their backs.

Thank you, Coach Gil Steinke!

Now, coming back to that advice about the hands you shake, I want to tell you the story of how I landed my first job after college. After playing football in the autumn of my sophomore year, I decided to let go of football so I could devote more time to my classes. With the challenging coursework, I just figured that if I were ever going to graduate, I needed to get more serious about studying.

Without football training and practice, I also had more time to work so I could earn extra money to cover my living expenses. I got a job as a maintenance manager for a couple of apartment complexes, and I steadily built up my responsibilities to the point where I was overseeing the maintenance of 188 apartment units. That gave me confidence in my potential to run a successful business of my own someday. But as I approached the finish line of earning my degree in range management, with my 2.7 GPA, I knew that I needed to go out and find a regular job.

Well, farming, ranching, wildlife—that's what I knew. The most natural fit I could land was a job offer with the federal government in the forestry arena. I can't remember exactly what I was going to be doing, probably watching deer in a pasture or something exciting like that. The starting pay was going to be $625 a month. It wasn't much, but it was a start.

Not long before my starting date, I happened to be attending my five-year Calhoun High School class reunion back home in Port Lavaca. As people were milling about, I noticed a guy named Martin Key who had graduated in the class ahead of mine. I knew him from our days playing high school football together, but he wasn't one of my best buddies and was a year older than me. It would have been easy to only hang out with those other guys all night, but I made a different choice. I went right over to Martin and shook his hand. After I asked him how things were going, Martin asked me something: "Now that you're graduating college, do you have your first job lined up yet?"

"Oh, yeah, I've got a job, and I think I'm going to be happy with it," I explained.

"Well, I just thought I'd let you know that I'm working for a company over in Alice, Texas, and we're hiring right now," Martin said. "I could help you get a job there if you think you might be interested. Of course, the starting salary is not that great. Just $1,250 a month."

"Oh, well then," I said with a mischievous grin, "maybe I'll just come on by and check that out."

Twice the starting salary as the wildlife job I was about to begin, and I "might" be interested? Are you kidding me?

This conversation occurred on a Saturday night, and the company was interviewing on Monday starting at 8 a.m. I got there by 6:30 and took my place first in line! I was offered a job almost right away with the Geo Vann Tool Company, earning double the income I expected to be making. All because I remembered Dr. Beran's advice to shake as many hands as possible, a lesson that I figured I should apply both to old friends and to people I was meeting for the first time.

My employer operated in the oil and gas industry. Basically, they helped provide the explosives needed when oil companies drilled oil wells. They told me they would teach me everything I needed to know, and they laid out the expected timetable for advancement. The first checkpoint was becoming a "specialist," which usually took a year or longer to achieve. Well, I was determined from the get-go to beat the clock on this kind of advancement and pay increase schedule.

Before I could execute that mission, however, I had to deal with a little bump in the road. At that time, I was living with my wife Cynthia, my childhood sweetheart, in a trailer park in Alice, a city of about 20,000, a half hour from Kingsville and forty-five miles from Corpus Christi.

I was in the middle of doing a few tasks for my job one morning on what happened to be my thirty-second day of my employment. That number was significant because my health insurance plan had just kicked in two days earlier. While building a small box, I set out to cut a V notch on a 2 × 4 on a table saw. While steadily guided along the ripping fence, the blade hit a knot in the 2 × 4, which launched the board over, along with my fingers, pulling them directly into the blade. The next thing I knew, I had cut through my fingers, leaving three of them hanging by the skin.

I was alone when this little mishap occurred. I didn't pass out. Didn't even scream. I had grown up surviving all kinds of injuries and accidents, and, like my mother said, when I found myself in the middle of some new adventure, I was always able to figure out what needed to be done to get out of it. So, I just supported the dangling fingers, holding on only by the skin, with my opposite hand, wrapped a rag around them, and went for help in my little Ford Courier pickup. I headed straight toward our mobile home and my wife.

"Do you know where the hospital is?" I shouted to her as I screeched to a halt in front of the trailer. We had only recently moved to Alice, and this was decades before cell phones and GPS.

"Yes, I drove by it the other day," she said. "What's wrong? What happened?"

"Oh, I just cut a few fingers off," I said calmly. As I spoke, I glanced down at my boot and noticed that it had already filled with blood.

She directed me as we raced to the hospital. When the ER staff examined me, they told me they would not be able to save my fingers. Strangely, one of my first thoughts was, *Dang, I guess I won't be able to play the guitar anymore.* That was something I had begun to really enjoy.

While I was still in the exam room, a doctor who appeared to be just walking by stopped to introduce himself. His name was Dr. Oaks; he lived in Canada, and he happened to be in the Alice area leading a seminar in his specialty: hand reconstruction!

"I believe I can reattach all your fingers," he said upon completing a thorough examination. "And since I'm leading a seminar here, would you mind if I allow some other doctors to observe the surgery?"

Heck, I wouldn't mind if he wanted to operate on me in a football stadium packed with doctors from all over the country, if it meant saving my fingers. Not long after this little coincidence, Dr. Oaks did his thing and got me all sewed up. All my fingers were neatly attached. I was overwhelmed with joy about the possibility of having my fingers back, but after a few weeks I noticed that all three fingers had begun to turn black on the ends.

"Oh, that's normal," the doctor explained. "Your blood supply was cut off. Don't worry, those black places will soon be coming off, just like a scab. And I bet you'll still be able to keep all your fingerprints."

Sure enough, my recuperation continued without a hitch. Still can't play the guitar, though.

My little accident at the table saw did not slow down my progress on the job. I became a specialist in ninety days, not the year that was predicted. After six months, they made me district manager.

I was advancing rapidly despite being new to the oil and gas industry. When I was growing up, oil wells had begun to pop up not far from us, but I wasn't one of those Texas kids who dreamed of becoming the next oil tycoon. Now here I was, just soaking up this world where it seemed like there was something new to learn every day! I also began to discover that, in many ways, once you get inside any industry, it's just like any other business. The goals are the same wherever you go, and the bottom line remains that you've got to do whatever you can to please your customers.

For me, the desire to earn more money and the curiosity to experiment with something new led me to try a side venture. I was playing softball with friends when I had an idea. Recreational softball was going gangbusters in Texas, and all those teams had to buy their equipment and their T-shirts somewhere. Maybe I could step in there in Alice and take advantage of this opportunity. That's how I came to be part of launching Sportabout, a store where we sold hats, balls, and other supplies for various sports teams. The biggest part of our operation came from the screen-printing equipment we had acquired. We wound up printing the T-shirts for most of the area's softball teams.

I started the store with my best friend Mike Maryan, whom I had gone to college with and who also had gotten a job with Vann. My wife Cynthia and a couple of other folks worked hard and kept the store afloat while I worked my day job. We weren't making a killing, but we did well enough for me to stick with it, even after my best friend decided to step out. I knew that this kind of business wasn't going to be my meal ticket, but I was already learning a lesson that I pass along today to other beginning entrepreneurs: Just because you may not feel like you have the "big vision" yet, there's no reason why you can't try to do something that you believe you can do well while experiencing a degree of success. When you do that, it will give you more confidence to go after the bigger opportunities when they come along later.

Meanwhile, I continued to excel in my work with Vann. From the start, I was fascinated by the process of using tools and explosives. I learned that setting up some kind of explosive downhole was not as complicated as  people from the outside might assume. After all, the military deals with explosives. So do bomb experts and many others. It was just a matter of figuring out how things work in this particular operation. Looked at that way, it wasn't all that different from figuring things out on the farm.

My advancement continued. A year after I was elevated to district manager, I was assigned to head up our company's new office in Oklahoma City. This was 1982, two years after the birth of my son Garrett. His brother Derrick came along in '84. During our transition to Oklahoma City, Cynthia and I sold Sportabout, which allowed us to put a down payment on a new house in a new development on the northwest side of Oklahoma City. This was a huge relief because for a while we thought we were going to have to drag our trailer house up there.

As a young man born and bred in Texas, if friends and family back home asked me to describe living in Oklahoma, I would say that it was like that license plate slogan: "Oklahoma is OK."

Similar to Texas, no matter where you went around Oklahoma, it felt like you never met a stranger. I liked that friendly atmosphere. We lived on a cul-de-sac in a neighborhood with lots of other kids, several of whom were close to Garrett's age.

Also, since I was now more rooted in the oil and gas industry, I found that it didn't really matter where you were living, as long as there was oil action around. Many of the people I was dealing with in Oklahoma were with the same companies I had been dealing with in Alice, Texas, and the new customers had the same attitude. Oil people were great people. Anytime you started talking oilfield, you just felt at home.

I found the weather a bit cooler than South Texas, but I could deal with that. The one thing I did miss was being close to water. I had enjoyed living near the Guadalupe River, the Victoria Barge Canal, and the bays and river bottoms that I had come to know back home. I have fond memories of going out fishing and waterskiing with my dad and brothers in his boat. Throughout my childhood, I had never been all that far from the Gulf Coast waters.

Fortunately, I discovered Lake Hefner, located right within the boundaries of Oklahoma City and not far from our home. Covering 2,500 acres, Lake Hefner was ideal for all kinds of boating, so when I heard about a guy selling his twenty-foot sailboat for an attractive price, I jumped right on it. Didn't matter a bit that I didn't know the first thing about sailing.

When I admitted this little stumbling block to my neighbor, he told me that he just happened to be an experienced sailor and agreed to start teaching me the very next day. I decided that I would bring Garrett along. After all, he was four years old, and boys should start enjoying and learning from adventures as early as possible, right?

I soon learned the basics of handling the rudder and hoisting up the mainsail, and I listened to my neighbor's explanation of how the wind would catch us and pull us this way and that way, and what tacking was all about. My teacher let me navigate for a while, and I was doing fine. In fact, I felt so smooth in handling my sailboat that when my neighbor guided us to the dock to wrap up my first lesson, I said confidently, "Well, I hope you enjoy the rest of your Saturday. I'm going back out."

"Oh, you're not ready to go solo yet," he warned. "There's a lot more to sailing than what I've shown you so far. You don't even have a motor that would allow you to come in if you got in any trouble."

He could have gone on for another hour trying to explain why I should wait for my next lesson, and it wouldn't have made one bit of difference to me. I had my mind made up. After I waved goodbye to my neighbor, I turned to Garrett.

"You want to have some FUN?" I asked.

"Yeah, Dad, I want to have some fun!" he exclaimed.

Off we went. First order of business was to raise the mast all the way up, not just to the halfway point my teacher had us stop at during my lesson. Zoom! We were really moving now. We were tacking and leaning, and everything was going just perfect until we began to approach a dam, with its 100-foot drop.

I knew enough to recognize that it was time to turn around. The trouble was, I had no idea how to do that. Yep, I had bitten off more than I could chew. In the midst of my frantic efforts to keep us from going over the dam, Garrett stuck his head up from the haul with tears in his eyes, he asked, "Dad, are we still having fun?" I guess you could say we were having a little "adventure."

Then, all of a sudden, still not knowing what to do as we were just about heading over the dam, I kicked all the sail ties loose to slow us down and, sure enough, the sail went over *that* way and my sailboat came about exactly as I needed it to. I had saved us in the nick of time! Like my mom would say, I just had a way of figuring things out, "but a little luck never hurt."

At work, I continued to become more and more accomplished in my role dealing with explosives and other tools that Vann provided to oil companies. I also kept my eyes open for other ways to supplement my income and try something new.

Believe it or not, I auditioned for a couple of modeling gigs while in Oklahoma City. Somebody just asked me if I would be willing to be featured in a photo spread for a rodeo. I guess they thought I fit the profile of the good-looking cowboy. For the first shoot, I wore a cowboy hat in downtown Oklahoma City. Then I did a shoot for Holiday Inn and one for J.C. Penney, and another one for the front cover of one of those apartment listing guides you grab when you move to a new location. My attitude in this new adventure was, "Hey, if you're going to pay me $35 an hour, I'll hang out anywhere you want me to." That little ride lasted about a year.

I was also still running my T-shirt business, mostly through my wife's efforts. Instead of operating out of a store, as we had done in Alice, Texas, we now printed the T-shirts right out of our garage.

We took on all kinds of orders. Living in Oklahoma, we had naturally become fans of the University of Oklahoma Sooners. The Sooners were contending for the '85 national football championship. It all came down to the season-ending game against Penn State in the Orange Bowl in Miami. In the buildup to this showdown, a business contact approached me with an offer. He wanted me to print 2,500 T-shirts declaring the Sooners as national champs—to be ready immediately after the Orange Bowl game was over. I got those T-shirts on consignment, understanding that I would use them to get printed up with the celebration message if Oklahoma won, or give them back to the vendor if they lost. I would cover the freight both ways.

The Sooners won the Orange Bowl 25–10; we cranked out the T-shirts in record time, and in accord with our deal, I sold the T-shirts to my contact for five bucks apiece. I think my profit was only $2 per shirt. Well, this guy turned around and sold the T-shirts that I had printed to all those celebrating Sooners' fans for $25 apiece. As I recall, he used his handsome profits to buy himself a new Corvette.

After this experience, I filed away a couple of lessons that I would call upon in the future:

- If you miss the mark on something that you try, just remember to keep learning, keep doing better, keep moving forward.
- Whenever and wherever possible, position yourself to be the lynchpin of any operation that you have a hand in, carving out a critical role for yourself and ensuring that you will reap the major rewards yourself.

CHAPTER 3

THE UNCOMMON MAN

You never know what's going to flip your trigger and ignite your work and career life.

When I talk to young people today, I advise them that it's important to find something that you really love, but it helps to keep in mind that this "something" may not show up for quite some time. And when it does come along, it could sweep you up and take you in a whole new direction, in a way that you would never expect.

Remember, I put my foot in the door of the oil and gas industry even though it had absolutely nothing to do with what I had been studying all through college. My decision to branch off and launch my own company in 1985 came about from another unexpected twist.

I guess you could say that what flipped my trigger to start a business—a business that I would one day sell for almost half a billion dollars—was the choice to spend a few hours one afternoon hanging out with a friend over a twelve-pack of beer. Let me explain:

I enjoyed my role of selling products and services that served the oil industry in my work for Vann, and I was so grateful for the opportunity to steer the company's new division in Oklahoma City in the early 1980s. But as I gained more and more experience, I found myself starting to come up with ideas for new tools that might perform some needed function for our customers more efficiently. Clients would describe something they really needed in their oilfield operation, and I would immediately begin sketching an idea on my favorite sketching material, which happened to be a napkin. It may sound silly, but I just liked napkins—they were just the right size, and they were usually found around a beer or two, which is where my creative juices really began to flow.

But I wasn't a professional designer or engineer. Nothing in my background had ever really taught me design skills. I did take a drafting class back in high school, but it wasn't a real passion for me at the time. I didn't like art classes all that much in school, and I had never been one of those kids who would take out a sketchbook or coloring book and easily entertain himself. But now I began having these ideas for tools that I might design. The question was, how could I turn my little design into a real, tangible representation that somebody could transform into a finished product that a customer would want to buy?

The answer started coming to me soon after my buddy Scott Hayes told me about AutoCAD. If you're not familiar with the term, AutoCAD is a computer-aided design and drafting software application that's still used today by engineers, graphic designers, architects, and other professionals. I always tried to keep an open mind about new possibilities, and Scott was enthusiastic about the program. I decided to check into what it would take to learn AutoCAD.

When I visited a vocational technology center, which just happened to be located directly behind our neighborhood, I discovered that they offered a class in AutoCAD. Great, I said, sign me up! Sorry, they said. In order to be accepted into this class, I would have to take a qualifying exam and then take what sounded like a bunch of other tests after that.

Whoa, I thought, there's got to be an easier way here. I called Scott, who was working in a profession where AutoCAD was commonly used. I explained about all the hoops I would have to jump through just to take a class to learn how to use AutoCAD.

"What should I do here?" I asked.

"Tell you what," said Scott, who lived in Dallas. "Drive down here and meet me at my place. Pick up a twelve-pack at the corner store, and by the time we get through that twelve-pack, I promise you that you will know how to use AutoCAD."

I had only one question for Scott before jumping in my pickup and hopping onto I-35 South for the three-hour drive to Dallas: "What kind of beer do you want me to buy?"

I paid strict attention during my one-afternoon crash course, while Scott was taking care of most of that twelve-pack. When he had finished with me, I had mastered the basics of AutoCAD well enough to rush right home, buy the program, and put it on my computer.

My trigger had just been flipped big-time!

It was like being five years old when you've just been given some new toy. I started designing ideas I was fiddling around with and was amazed at how good this program made them look. The details were so precise it was like magic! It almost felt like I had gone back to school to learn a whole new trade. Before long, I was able to graduate to more and more complicated designs. I was literally staying up all night sometimes, just exploring the many applications of AutoCAD and dreaming about how I could put them all to use.

It didn't take long to take my dream and turn it into reality. I was talking with my customer with one of our clients, Texas Oil & Gas, when he mentioned a certain kind of tool that could really improve their operation, something that would perform in a different way than the tool they currently used. I listened closely, went back to my AutoCAD, and drew what I hoped would be their solution. When I showed it to my customer a few days later, he had a one-word response: "Perfect!" I guess my presentation seemed a little more credible than a napkin and a few beers!

I was excited to show my design to my boss at Vann. His response? "We'll have to bring it to our engineering department and see what they think." When word came back from the engineers, their verdict was clear: It's not going to work. Can't do the job. Forget about it. And anyway, I wasn't even an engineer.

At first, I felt devastated. I really thought I had something worthwhile to offer with my new design skills. And if I did, who knows where that might take me?

When I reported the disappointing news to my Texas Oil & Gas customer, he listened patiently. Then he leaned in closer to me.

"Lynn, if you build this tool, we'll buy it from you," he said. "Not only that; we'll use it on every one of our oil wells."

Well, that was a great vote of confidence! Now I just had to figure out how I was going to take my hot new design and actually produce it. That wasn't something I could do myself, and it's not like I had a ready-made production staff standing by waiting for me to begin my own operation.

Fortunately, I had continued to follow that advice from my college chemistry professor to shake as many hands as I could. I had made a lot of friends, and one of them, Bill Bishop, ran a machine shop. I felt a little anxious explaining my dilemma to him, but I was determined. I really believed that if I could just cross over this one hurdle and make this tool into something real, I would be on the verge of something new and exciting in my career.

It helped that even before this meeting, I had begun showing Bill some of my designs that I would draw on napkins, or maybe a piece of paper. He and his two sons would patiently sit with me and tell me how to draw my idea in a way they could understand better. Now, thanks to AutoCAD, I was bringing him a much more polished design.

"Lynn, I'll tell you what I'll do for you," Bill said. "I'll build twelve of these new tools for you. No charge. When you get paid for selling them, you can pay me then. How's that sound?"

How's that sound? Good enough for me to take the leap and start my own business!

And that's how my dream of Magnum was born in May 1985. My trigger got flipped just by learning about some computer program that I had never even known existed until a friend told me about it. A spark was ignited. I just followed the blazing trail from there.

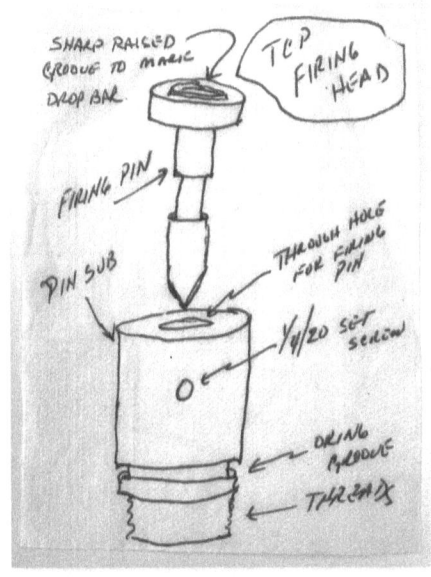

Of course, I did have to take care of a few practical considerations before making the commitment to go off on my own. Or at least, somewhat practical. I approached a few other oil companies to assess their potential interest in purchasing my new tool, direct from me with this new company that I was planning to launch, and I received a very enthusiastic response. When I began to assess my profit margin, I saw the potential to be making $3,000–$4,000 for one day of work. That looked pretty darn good to me!

Then I thought of the vast potential throughout the giant oil industry that I had been successfully navigating for several years already. I figured there ought to be a great opportunity to sell my new tool right there in Oklahoma and a ton of potential in Texas, where I knew the landscape and had some potentially helpful contacts. And with the dominance of the oil industry in those days, I just figured I would find hot pockets of activity in dozens of locations all over the country. Maybe even beyond U.S. borders.

Yes, there was so much business out there to be gained. And the area of products and services I was focusing on was part of the new technology. It really seemed like everybody would want it. I figured that I didn't need to draw up a complete A-to-Z business plan to jump into action.

"I have to do this!" I said to myself.

I launched my business, full of enthusiasm and confidence about my possibilities for big-time success. I was really following my dream to make my customer a hero!

Of course, I still had moments when the reality of taking this big plunge felt scary. I knew that most business start-ups didn't make it, and I was a husband and a dad with a four-year-old and a one-year-old to provide for.

My wife and I were still running the T-shirt business in our garage, so that was helpful as a secondary revenue stream. We were printing T-shirts for some of the fraternities at OU (Oklahoma University), as well as for a few golf companies, and even for Walmart and C.R. Anthony Co., the big Oklahoma department store. But I knew that I needed to get myself and my new business out there as quickly and aggressively as possible.

Fortunately, my best friend from college, Mike Maryan, lived in Corpus Christi and was well connected in the area. That helped open doors back in South Texas. I called upon another friend, Dale Seekford in Shreveport, Louisiana, to create some jobs for me there. Soon I would be extending into Kansas, Colorado, and beyond.

Unfortunately, that all didn't happen overnight. In 1986, just a year or so into the operation of Magnum, I ran right smack into one of the downturns that seem to come along in the oil industry from time to time. In that year, the price of oil dropped by more than half. A book titled *Belly Up: The Collapse of the Penn Square Bank* by Phillip L. Zweig provides an excellent backstory of the impact on this downturn in Oklahoma City. But we didn't need to read any book to know what happened; the Frazier household took a direct hit.

So, there I was: I had quit my job with Vann and had started down the road of my dreams, but I still had house payments, car payments, electric bills, and a whole lot more to keep paying. And now I had all these new business expenses to manage. I had a family to support, with Garrett five years old and Derrick two years old when the downturn hit. Money was tight, very tight. As I look back at that challenging time, there is one day that tells the story of my experience better than any words ever could.

My wife Cynthia approached me and said, "We need milk for Derrick, and there's no money in the checkbook."

This was a real jolt. My two-year-old son needed milk, and my wife was telling me we couldn't afford it! I opened up my wallet—nothing. Next, I frantically reached for the spare coin jar on the dresser. All I could scrounge up there were four nickels and three pennies. That wasn't going to do the job. Running out of the house, I headed straight for my car. Popping up the back seat, I found a few more coins, enough to at least buy a half gallon of milk.

Things got a little better after that day, but it was still a struggle for a while. Somehow, we managed to keep our home and our family afloat. But even in the midst of those struggles, I was determined not only to make my new business work well enough to keep putting food on the table but also to take time for our family to enjoy ourselves.

One Saturday afternoon, I believe it was in July 1986, we had a group of friends and neighbors over at our house for a little get-together. Everyone there knew that times were pretty tough financially for me and my family, but on this day we were all just having a good time. We shared great food and lots of drinks, and we had a few good laughs.

The gathering rolled into the evening hours, and at some point, I was asked about my oilfield business and my hopes and dreams for the future. I admitted that I was finding that my dream came with its share of challenges. To illustrate my point, I told them the whole story of that day when I had to flip the car seat just to come up with enough coins to buy milk for our little one.

Before I could finish my story, one of the ladies chimed in, "Lynn, why don't you just quit this business and go get your old job back? Forget about this oilfield dream. Then you can take care of your family."

For one long moment, I felt a bit flustered. I was among friends, people who I thought would be supportive of me and what I was trying to do. I wasn't expecting to be blindsided like that. I took a minute to gather my thoughts: This was devastating . . .

Finally, I cleared my throat and nodded at this woman, who I'm sure had good intentions. Then I looked out over the gathering of our other neighbors and friends.

"Guys, you just watch," I said firmly. "I've got a feeling about these oilfield tools I'm making. I really believe that one of these days I'm gonna have tools in oilfields not just in Oklahoma and Texas but all over the world." I smiled real big before continuing, "Yes, I am confident that I will be a real contender in this industry one day."

After I spoke, everything got very, very quiet. For what seemed like a minute, or even two, everybody just looked at one another. No one was saying anything. I was expecting, or maybe just hoping, that at least one or two folks would speak up and tell me that they believed in me, that they knew I was going to make it. But that's not what happened. Instead, they all started roaring with laughter. They thought it was a joke!

I just sat there, unable to speak, wanting to crawl into a hole. This was my dream that everyone was laughing at! I just couldn't believe that other people, even some folks who knew me pretty well, thought the idea of me leading a successful business in the oil and gas industry was crazy.

I'm not sure exactly what I said or did during the rest of that party. But I do remember I was saying to myself, "I'll show them!" Other people may not have had confidence in me and what I was trying to do, but I did. I lay awake most of the night, deep in thought, not knowing what I should do. Finally, I made a vow to myself:

My company, Magnum, will one day set the standard for quality design and performance for downhole completion tools in the oilfield industry. And I will find awesome people to help me nourish and accomplish this goal!

Over the next thirty-plus years, that is exactly what we did.

That's the kind of determination that you feel when you have waited for that one inspired idea that flips your trigger and gives you the fuel to keep powering on.

As I began to establish myself on more solid ground with my new company, and the oil downturn slowly began to take a turn for the better, I was listening to the needs of my network and my customers, and helping them by coming up with all kinds of new ideas. Some of these ideas related to designing tools, but I also had some creative plans for going out and selling our tools and services. Here's one idea that really clicked:

If you were around in the 1980s, you might remember the popular TV show *Magnum, P.I.* The show chronicled the exploits of Thomas Magnum, a private investigator in Hawaii. The lead character was played by Tom Selleck, the handsome actor known in that role for his red Ferrari convertible, his colorful Hawaiian shirts, and his big, sweeping mustache.

Right from the start, I was well aware of our company's link to the show's name. And yeah, a *few* people even said I looked a bit like Tom Selleck, especially since my mustache, which I still maintain today, was bigger and bushier back then. So, I figured, why not make the link to the TV show a little more direct?

My plan began with my first business card. When I launched my company, I used the name Magnum Services. As part of my new campaign, I changed the name to Magnum *Petro* Services Incorporated. When I designed our business card, I put the name "Magnum" all in red. Then I also used red for the "P" in Petro Services and the "I" in Incorporated. My idea was that from a distance, or at a quick glance, all anyone would see was this:

Magnum P.I.

I wasn't done there. I bought a red Hawaiian shirt and a pair of jeans that were as close as I could find to what Tom Selleck wore on TV. Finally, I ordered a large box of little red Ferrari Hot Wheels.

Now I was ready to start doing some in-person cold-calling to drum up business. Up until that time, if I had tried to walk into the office of an oil and gas company without an appointment, I wouldn't get past the secretary's desk. Now, as I sought out new prospects, I would have a new calling card backing me up. Yes sir, Tom Selleck would have my back.

"Hello, I'm here to see so-and-so," I would announce to the woman behind the reception desk. "It's very important."

As I spoke those words, I would hand her my business card with the Magnum P.I., and right on top of that business card, I had placed one of my little red Ferrari Hot Wheels. I made sure that she couldn't take one without the other.

"Oh, yes, sir," the woman would say. "I'll be right with you."

Flashing my big smile, I'd like to think she picked up on my resemblance to Tom Selleck. Even if she didn't, I figured she would somehow be thinking of the TV show and that this would help her see that, yes, I really *was* important.

Sure enough, within minutes I would be invited in to see some high-level executive at this company I was hoping to win over. And, almost every time, the woman who had opened the gate for me to come inside her company would ask me one little question: "What would you like me to do with this cute little car?"

"Oh, you can keep the car," I would say, flashing that big smile again. Then, when that same secretary would greet me on my return calls, she would not just nod professionally and say, "Hello, Mr. Frazier." She would also break into a wide grin and say, "Hey, Magnum!"

New jobs were popping up all over: Kansas, Arkansas, Central Texas, the Panhandle. I was actually able to start hiring staff. For a time, I had a couple of guys who could run the jobs on-site while my little red Ferrari Hot Wheels and I focused on sales. I would listen carefully to each new client, then go back and design or modify a tool to fulfill this customer's needs. I continued working with Bill Bishop to produce the tools that I designed. Then I brought on board a few salesmen, sending one to Dallas, one to Wichita or Tulsa or wherever they were needed.

Bill and his sons were always willing to offer me advice or guidance about designing. They helped me understand how everything was done in calculations, they showed me how to pick out the right materials, and they taught me other fine points of the engineering process. It was great that I had learned my way around a key program like AutoCAD, but I understood that if I was really going to make my mark engineering, designing, and selling new tools for the oilfield industry, I would have to constantly build on my knowledge base.

In those early years, staff would come and go. A few of my new hires joined us after also leaving Vann. I had helpers, but I have to admit that there were many days when it felt like I had to do *everything* myself: make the sales calls, design the tools, then go out and run the job on-site, only to return to the shop, clean up, and prepare for the next job. That didn't faze me, though. I knew that it would take time to build the foundation of my company. We just had to keep moving forward.

It helped that I wasn't primarily driven by the financial part of growing a business. Don't get me wrong; I sure never wanted to find myself back in the position of flipping my car seat to scrounge up milk money. Mostly, though, I was steered by inspiration and aspiration. I was inspired to pursue my dream, and I just aspired to go higher, to do more, to do better. I knew there was more out there for Magnum, and I just wanted to keep moving forward and taking the next steps to go find it.

To me, this drive was like finding yourself on a very steep set of stairs. You just wanted to keep climbing those stairs, no matter how many there seemed to be.

I never had a real plan B. I just believed in what I was doing. I knew that the tools and services that I was designing and selling were needed, that we were part of something that was growing and evolving, and that I was growing and evolving right along with it. It just all seemed to fit together. To use another analogy, one that my uncles Anthony and Ricky would have appreciated, I was just going to keep flying this same airplane and see where it took me.

Like that flight director said during the Apollo 13 mission, failure was not an option. That was the attitude that I had carried with me back when I was a college freshman, battling to earn a place on the Texas A&I football team as a walk-on and then setting out to impress my coaches enough to be awarded a full scholarship. And now, with Magnum, failure again was not an option. I was just going to do whatever I needed to do and ride through any storm that came crashing into my path.

That meant being resourceful about office space for my new company. Starting out, I just ran my operation out of my garage at home. After a while, I could afford to rent an office space in a strip mall. Then, after moving to a new home in Oklahoma City, I came up with another idea. I bought a Sea-Can container and set it up on our property. I built some shelves and workbenches inside and kept adding more touches to this 8 × 8 × 40–foot space so it would fit my needs. Then I set up our two-car garage with a shop to test out the tools that I would design and take to my builder to construct. We also constructed a console with a "test well" where we were able to replicate and monitor downhole pressures and temperatures.

One way or another, I was doing what needed to be done, following my dream and my unwavering commitment to aspire for something higher.

I was not the kind of young businessman who would read a lot of how-to-do-it business books for advice. I couldn't have told you the names of the latest best-selling inspirational authors that everybody was gushing about. But now and then I would come across some simple quotation with an idea or a feeling that would make me say, "Yeah, that's what I believe!" It wouldn't matter to me who said it or when. If the words rang true to me, I just took it to heart.

During those early years of running Magnum in Oklahoma, I was especially drawn to a short verse that I always referred to as "The Uncommon Man." I only found out much later that this quotation came from Dean Alfange, who had been a lawyer and politician in New York City. His politics sounded way too liberal for me, but what he said in this verse just made sense to me. I guess a lot of other people must have felt the same way because his piece was published in the 1950s in *Reader's Digest*, where it was referred to as "An American Creed."

> *I do not choose to be a common man. It is my right to be uncommon. I seek to develop whatever talents God gave me—not security. I do not wish to be a kept citizen, humbled and dulled by having the state look after me. I want to take the calculated risk; to dream and to build, to fail and to succeed. I refuse to barter incentive for a dole. I prefer the challenges of life to the guaranteed existence; the thrill of fulfillment to the stale calm of utopia. I will not trade freedom for beneficence nor my dignity for a handout. I will never cower before any earthly master nor bend to any threat. It is my heritage to stand erect, proud and unafraid; to think and act myself, enjoy the benefit of my creations and to face the world boldly and say—'This, with God's help, I have done.' All this is what it means to be an American.*

I decided to quote some of his phrases, modify others, and write my own creed based on his to hang up in my office. Here is my own modified version of Mr. Alfange's creed:

I DO NOT CHOOSE TO BE A COMMON MAN.

It is my right to be uncommon—if I can. I seek opportunity—
not security. I do not wish to be a kept citizen, humbled and
dulled by having a company look after me.

I want to take the calculated risk; to dream
and to build, to fail and to succeed.

I refuse to barter incentive for a dole. I prefer the
challenges of life to the guaranteed existence; the thrill
of fulfillment to the stale calm of utopia.

It is my heritage to stand erect, proud, and unafraid;
to think and act for myself, enjoy the benefits of my creations,
and to face the world boldly and say, this I have done.

Reading those words, I just felt a stronger belief that nothing was going to hold me back. Some people might prefer to patiently sit and keep doing what they had always known, but I just wasn't built that way. As the creed says, I felt driven "to dream and to build."

I may not have had a big staff to share my version of "An American's Creed" with, but I did have two growing boys. From the time that Garrett and Derrick were young, I wanted to show them what their dad was doing in his professional life. I figured I could introduce them to simple tasks they could perform for Magnum, even if it was only cleaning up the shop after a long day's work.

I had big hopes for Garrett and Derrick, as most fathers do for their sons. Like the words from that creed, I wanted them to grow up to build something so that they too could enjoy the benefits of their creations. Maybe, just maybe, it would work out someday that Magnum would be much bigger and more successful, and my two boys would choose to share in the challenges and rewards with me.

In the meantime, I just wanted to do what I could to bring them into my world. One day, when Garrett was about nine and Derrick five, I walked them into my Sea-Can shop and showed them around. I pointed out my copy of "I Do Not Choose to Be a Common Man."

"That's what I'm doing in here," I said. "This is why I'm in business."

They may not have understood everything in the verse, but I helped translate it for them so they could get the basic meaning in their own way. Then I had another idea, and I guided them back to the office to my Xerox machine.

"Okay," I said, "now I want you both to put your hands down on the screen together."

They might have laughed a little, but they did as I suggested. As soon as their hands were properly in place, I laid my own hand right down on top of theirs. Then I pushed the copy button.

Garrett and Derrick eagerly reached toward the tray to pull out the copy. And there it was: the Frazier men, hand in hand in hand. As I took an extra moment to look over this image, I smiled. "You see, boys," I said, "I've got you covered. Always remember that."

I tucked that Xerox copy in a drawer. As the years rolled by, each time I would move into some new office space, I made sure that copy stayed with me in my desk. I happen to be a bit of a hoarder (some who know me might say that's a big understatement!), but I'll tell you one of the advantages of being a hoarder: I still have that Xerox copy today.

And after all that my boys and I have been through together, that piece of paper has taken on layers and layers of meaning for me.

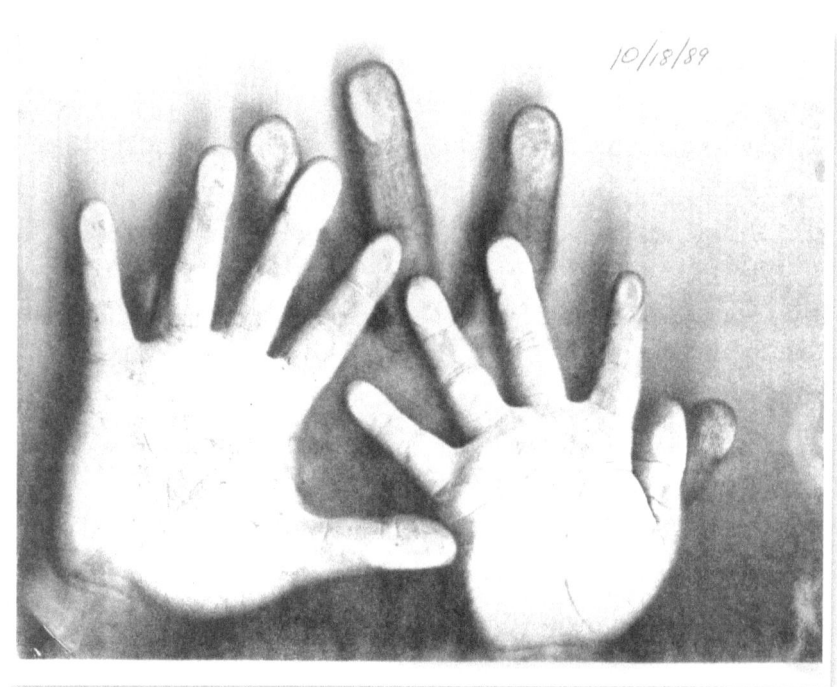
10/18/89

CHAPTER 4

FOLLOW THE OIL

I can't remember where I picked up my old-fashioned treasure chest, but I always enjoy showing it to anyone who visits me in my new office in Corpus Christi. I keep that chest filled with dozens and dozens of coins that I have collected while traveling the world. Each coin carries memories of some experience I will never forget.

The coins are real currency from a wide variety of countries and cultures: Mexico, Colombia, Venezuela, Belize, Egypt, China, Vietnam, Australia, New Zealand. Those are just some of the places where I have spent many days, weeks, or even months over the span of a couple of decades.

And make no mistake, I wasn't hunkering down in those faraway locations as a tourist. Sometimes I did manage to spare a little time to take in a few of those popular destinations we all hear about, but I was mostly there with a serious purpose. Oil companies were setting up in those countries because they had to follow the trail of oil wherever it took them all across the globe. And for Magnum to succeed, I had to follow the guys who were following the oil.

I can tell you there's a big difference between hopping over to some new country for fun and arriving there because you're helping to run the explosives in some oil well. The biggest difference is that you're working long and hard hours to get the job done, but you're also pretty likely to find yourself standing knee-deep in some wild and crazy, and sometimes dangerous situations. At least that was true for me.

Follow the Oil

I'm not complaining. Since I survived each and every one of those crazy times, I get to tell the story of how I made it.

First, it will be helpful to back up in time and paint a little bit of the picture of what was happening in the oil and gas industry during my first phase of establishing and growing Magnum. If you weren't yet born in the 1980s, or you just weren't tuned into the world of oil and gas at that time, you may not be aware of how U.S.-based oil companies were turning more and more to foreign countries in their pursuit of oil and gas exploration opportunities.

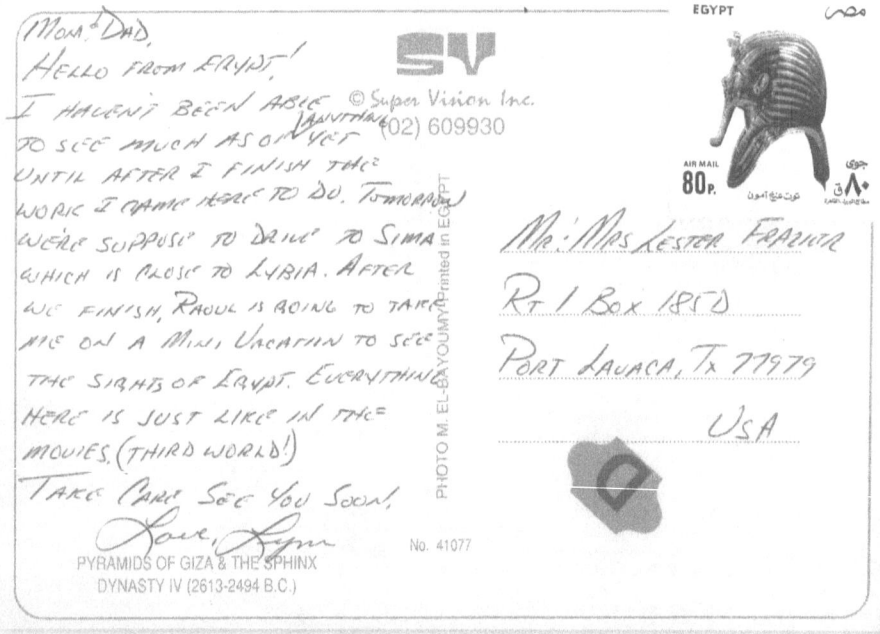

If you glanced at the news headlines, you were probably aware that the Middle East was a major focus of producing and buying the oil used in our country. Middle Eastern oil activity definitely had a major impact on our energy supply and our political activity during that time, and, like anyone who has committed to serving the oil and gas industry, I spent my share of time in the Middle East. But what many people don't know is that if you were following the trail of oil in the late twentieth century, you were probably going to find yourself in many other regions and countries as well. Oil was being discovered and produced in large quantities in some places you might never have imagined. And I was heading right into those places, wherever they happened to be.

I didn't have a choice. If I really wanted Magnum to become as successful as my dreams, I would need to expand my horizons beyond Oklahoma, Texas, Louisiana, Kansas, Colorado, and other U.S. locations where I had been operating with my cutting-edge tools and products. I would need to get out there and start doing some serious traveling.

The door began to open for me while I was attending an oil show in

Houston in 1989. I met an agent who was very interested in my tools and equipment related to the use of explosives in oil and gas exploration and production. This agent, Wayne Tucker, lived and worked in Trinidad, where he and his family successfully operated The Tucker Group, a formidable service company. At that time, Amoco was doing offshore work in Trinidad, an island just off the coast of Venezuela, and through this agent I was extended an invitation to bring my equipment there and start running jobs in support of Amoco's work. I jumped at the chance. This was just the kind of opportunity to expand into non-U.S. markets that I was seeking.

Due to the mismanagement of a larger service company, we had our chance to prove ourselves with our innovative technology. Now I've got to tell you that when you're handling the explosives for an offshore oil rig, you're sweating it out every minute. With the bottom of that well 10,000 feet below the sea floor, you had to make sure that all your measurements and everything else involved in the operation were perfect or ... well, you couldn't afford to even imagine the consequences if anything went wrong. Fortunately, everything went off the way it was supposed to, and we were awarded a two-year contract with the help of our International Salesman, Lloyd Stock. Not only that, but I was also invited to fly over to Venezuela where I would be introduced to some other folks interested in what Magnum offered. Sounded good to me.

I left Trinidad in a private plane with Wayne, my partner on these projects. The plan was to fly into Caracas, the capital city of Venezuela with a population of around two million and a decent-sized airport. But when we were told that the weather was not conducive to landing in Caracas, our flight had to be rerouted. We would land instead in Barcelona, drive south to Anaco, and then finally on to Caracas. That was actually closer to Trinidad, so it seemed convenient, and I trusted that they could arrange the follow-up transportation we would need to get from Barcelona to Caracas to meet my potential client.

Follow the Oil

The only problem was that Barcelona, a much smaller city, didn't exactly have the same kind of facilities as Caracas. Apparently, small private planes needed some kind of formal clearance to land, and it just so happened that we didn't have that proper clearance.

So there we were, taxiing to a stop as military jeeps charged toward us. We managed to get out of the plane and were in the process of hustling into a car waiting on the tarmac to pick us up.

"Don't worry, we're just going to drive around those guys. Everything will be okay," Wayne and our driver blurted out.

But before I could even slide into the "getaway" car, one of those soldiers bolted out of his jeep, grabbed me, and pushed me, hard, against our little private plane. Then he stuck a gun in my back and said something in a harsh voice. I had learned enough Spanish by then to understand the general idea: "You, go over there!"

I flashed Wayne a frightened what-do-I-do-now look.

"Just do whatever he tells you!" Wayne exclaimed, and then he closed the door to the car I was supposed to be safely sitting in. Questions swirled in my head: *Do what, and go where? And what is this guy with the gun in my back going to do to me when I get there?*

But I had no choice. The soldier marched me toward a little room in a nearby building and motioned for me to sit down. He had that gun still pointed right at me. We just remained that way, in our little Venezuelan standoff, for what seemed like two terrifying hours but was probably closer to two minutes. Finally, Wayne and the driver of the car that had met our plane pulled up to the building they were keeping me in. He jabbered at the soldiers in Spanish and then signaled for me to join him.

"Sheesh, Wayne," I said once we were in the clear, "what the heck was going on back there? I was so damn scared I could have been shot! And who were those guys?"

"Oh, them?" he said with a grin. "Those guys were just fifteen-year-old military guys in training. They didn't even let them have bullets." And then

65

he laughed. "We just need to pay them so they can get their beer money." (About $1,500 USD.)

Experiences like that one taught me very quickly that running jobs in other countries, whether offshore or on land, required more than just making sure you did excellent work. You also had to successfully navigate the culture and the habits of people in the country you were doing business in. Since my business prospects, not to mention my personal survival, were at stake, I knew that I would have to stay on my toes at all times.

Even when I was able to block out a little free time to explore some new country that I found myself in, it seemed like some scary moment was waiting for me around every bend. I remember that time in Nigeria when I had half a day to kill between meetings related to some potential work with Grace Petroleum.

I was staying in a house on a river when a local Nigerian came by in a little motorboat that could barely carry the three of us and offered my partner and me a tour of the area. "How much?" we asked. "Five dollars, whole day," he answered. I grabbed my video camera and was having a great time in the boat, shooting video of the monkeys jumping around in the trees as we motored up the river deeper into the jungle.

When I spotted a group of Nigerian fishermen casting their grass-woven fishing nets from a pier, I asked our boat driver to pull over. With the sight of me pointing my camera capturing everybody's attention, one of the guys approached me and demanded money. My camera was chasing the spirits away and sabotaging their catch, he said. I took out a couple of $10 bills to cool him off. After we tied off the boat to give him the money, a couple of Nigerian teenagers came rushing down the pier, waving us up to come see the Mmanwu, a traditional Nigerian masquerade ceremony performed only by males to invoke the ancestral spirits.

We were always up for a little adventure, so we followed these teenagers to meet the chief of the local village, who extended his official invitation for me to attend the Mmanwu. He even told me I could take my camera with me. I followed him, and when we arrived, about fifty local kids came right up to me and rubbed my arm, I guess because they were fascinated to see somebody with white skin. The chief gave me his okay to videotape the local men dancing in their grass skirts and beating their drums in a circle, but a few minutes into their performance, two big guys in black slacks and white shirts crept up on either side of me and began to tug at my camera. Feeling very confused, I looked at the chief.

"You must leave our village . . . now!" said the chief, who, I noticed, happened to be standing over my shoulder.

Well, you didn't have to tell me twice. I yanked the camera out of the guard's hand and ran back to the motorboat. We were gone!

At least I got away with my video camera.

I was fast learning that wherever I traveled, anything I carried with me, not to mention my own safety, could be at risk. Another story that reminds me of how true that was will take us back to South America.

While in Venezuela, I heard about opportunities in the neighboring country of Colombia. If my memory of this little adventure is correct, I was returning to Venezuela from Colombia. I had traveled by air going over to Colombia, but apparently there were no available flights for the return. That meant driving farther south to a point where we could cross the border by car.

We got stuck in a long line at the crossing, and I noticed right away that the border guards were flagging quite a few cars for further searching. Sure enough, when they spotted me in my business attire of suit and tie, they thought I looked suspicious. Or maybe they just thought that I made for a good target for their "searches."

A couple of guards ordered me to get out of the car and walk over to a building where they escorted me into a small room. I understood that I would be waiting in that room while they rummaged through my luggage and other possessions in the room next door. And I would not be waiting in my suit and tie.

"Strip . . . to your underwear," I was told.

After I had complied, I was led into a larger adjoining room, where they patted me down from head to toe. I'm sure they had uncovered their share of drug smugglers with this maneuver, but I had a pretty good idea that wasn't what they thought was going on with me. I was mostly thinking about the $5,000 in $100 bills stored with my luggage. Proving that I was not totally naïve about such matters, I had distributed those $100 bills throughout the pages of a book that I had packed in the suitcase that I had bought in Colombia.

At least the border officials were not screaming at me. They just kept repeating the same questions over and over: "Do you have any money? Are you carrying any cash?"

"No, no," I kept responding. When they had finished searching me, and apparently my luggage too, they escorted me back to the little room where I had gotten undressed.

"Get dressed and go," I was told.

They looked very disappointed. As I put my pants back on, I noticed that the two $20 bills I had tucked in my pocket were gone. No surprise there. But when I had safely gotten well past the border, I went looking for my little book. Whew! Every $100 bill was still in there, right where I had placed them. All I could think was that if they had ever found that cash, I would have lost a whole lot more than five thousand bucks. It was just one more episode where I had escaped, alive and pretty much unharmed.

I maintained an office for Magnum in Venezuela for a few years until I discovered that my equipment was being copied. Around this time, Hugo Chavez was about to take over the country, causing major political unrest and unstable conditions for foreigners. As a result, my opportunity, along with the country, began to crumble; time to pull up stakes again.

Although I always managed to escape these situations in faraway countries, those who happened to be accompanying me were not always so lucky. I was pursuing prospects in Thailand one time when I found myself sitting in the back seat of a taxi, my luggage at my side. I had just been picked up from the airport for the drive to my hotel. The way I remember it, I had a business appointment scheduled there and needed to arrive without delay. And, of course, a delay is just what we drove into.

Our taxi wound up at the front of a long line of traffic held up by Thai police officers for some unknown reason. There never did seem to be any explainable reason for all kinds of delays, rerouting, searches, and other incidents I seemed to stumble into during my travels.

I had explained my time crunch to the taxi driver, and he was doing his best to make it happen. He began to carefully ease his car around the cop holding up traffic. I was thinking to myself, *I don't know if I need to get to the meeting bad enough to piss off a Thai police officer.*

In the next few seconds, our taxi bumped into that cop. Not enough to injure him, so far as I could tell, but enough to get him riled up. So riled up that he walked up to the taxi driver's window, pulled out his pistol, and shot him, blood spattering me in the backseat!

I didn't need a translator to tell me that it wasn't going to be safe for me to sit in the back of that taxi waiting to see how all this was going to be sorted out. Terrified, I opened the door to that taxi with my right hand, grabbed my suitcase with my left hand, and took off running. Never even slammed the door behind me.

"I could be a goner this time for sure!" I muttered to myself.

I ran and I ran, and I didn't stop for the twenty minutes it took me to get to my hotel. I tried to catch my breath and straighten up my clothes before checking in, so as not to arouse suspicion, and I made it to my meeting on time.

I never did hear anything about what that traffic holdup was all about, and I don't even know what happened to my poor taxi driver. Working in some of these far-off places, you learned not to ask many questions.

It didn't always take a cop, a soldier, or a border guard to start something that left me in a dangerous situation. Sometimes it could be someone who appeared entirely harmless.

That's the way it happened one day while I was working on an oil project in Egypt. I was leaving Cairo and heading to a little town close to the Libyan border. The Egyptian-Libyan border was known as a major danger zone during those days, but I never figured that a donkey cart would be the source of danger that we ran into.

I had a driver to transport me to my destination. When we reached one particular area, I noticed a lot of donkey carts tying up traffic on our road. Suddenly, a kid, probably no older than eight or nine, pulled right in front of us in one of those donkey carts. He appeared to be trying to cross the road, but he wasn't anywhere near any intersection. All he really seemed to be accomplishing was to block our path.

My driver began honking his horn and yelling at this kid to get out of the road. The boy and his donkey cart, however, were hardly moving.

By this time, all the noise my driver was making had attracted the attention of a bunch of ladies in this town we were driving through. Dressed in their burkas, they began storming out of nearby buildings and picking up rocks. Taking careful aim, they fired those rocks toward our car. As soon as a rock busted one of our windows, my driver turned to me.

"Run!" he shouted, and he pointed in the direction he believed would be safe for me to go. Again, when you're caught in one of these situations, you don't stop to ask questions. So once again I was on the run, not from cops or soldiers but from a gang of burka-clad, rock-throwing Egyptian women!

Eventually, I reached what appeared to be safe ground. A half hour later, my driver walked up to meet me. He guided me to the hotel I had reserved and got me checked in so I could clean up. This time, I was willing to return to the scene of the crime. I walked with my driver to the spot where I had fled from our car, keeping my eyes peeled for any remaining signs of those raging ladies.

What a scene! Every window of our car had been smashed, and all the tires punctured. From what I could understand and what my driver explained, those ladies just didn't think it was right for us to be honking and hollering at that boy the way we did. And they were more than willing to hammer out our punishment right there on the spot.

Yes, sir, in those days of international travel to pursue business opportunities for Magnum, there was never a dull moment. Sometimes I came home with more than just another wild story to tell. I would also walk away, alive and intact, with some new idea that I might apply in my own life several years or even decades later.

To explain, I need to tell a story that takes us back to Colombia.

I was with one of my Colombian partners, Jaime, at the time, and while I was working one project in Colombia, he told me about potential interest in us doing a job with British Petroleum. To meet them, he had to drive me from Bogota in the central region of Colombia to Cali, closer to the Pacific coast.

It was a beautiful drive through the hills of Colombia. While I relaxed for an hour or so, I was able to appreciate that when I wasn't running to escape some dangerous situation in all these fascinating countries, I would have moments like this one, when I really could stop to admire the stunning scenery.

Out in the countryside, off the main highway, our car pulled up to a beautiful gold, stucco house with a six-car garage. I loved the color, and the whole structure was pretty impressive. I figured that whoever owned a place like that in Colombia must have been doing pretty darn well for himself.

Just as I was fully absorbing the spectacle before me, the time to relax came to an abrupt end. A bunch of guys came running out of that great big gold-colored house, and they were not empty-handed.

"Let's get out of here!" I shouted to Jaime when I spotted their machine guns.

"No, don't worry," Jaime said. "These guys, they're just some friends of mine."

I wasn't 100 percent convinced right away, so when one of these "friends" ran right to the side of our car, his machine gun at his hip, I ducked down onto the seat and lay still in a crouched position. It was only after I spotted Jaime hugging his buddy that I dared to sit up.

"Come on, they just want to show us inside the house," Jaime said.

As I followed him, I kept darting my eyes around for signs of danger. As our little welcoming committee opened two doors to the huge, six-car garage, I gasped. All I could see were pallets and pallets, each about four feet by four feet tall, filled with stacks of money. I didn't have to strain my eyes to see that the stacks were all $100 bills.

Jaime smiled, picked up one of the stacks, and tossed it to me. I tried my best NOT to catch the money. I still wasn't sure what danger might be lurking inside this little hideaway. I also made sure that the guys in this big gold house noticed that I was carefully stooping down to retrieve those $100 bills and placing them neatly back in the pile.

"The guy who owns this house has about six hundred houses all over the country," Jaime explained. I didn't have to guess the identity of this big-money homeowner: Pablo Escobar, the notorious Colombian drug lord. This was during the time that Escobar's multibillion-dollar drug cartel controlled most of the cocaine traffic heading into the United States. That pretty much would explain those pallets of money.

After this little show staged for my benefit was over, we drove away and got on with our own business, which, fortunately, was all about oil, not illegal drugs. But it would not be the last time I heard Pablo Escobar's name. While I was still working in Colombia, the DEA was closing in on Escobar. From what I heard, Escobar apparently didn't want to get caught with all the goods, so he blew up dozens of the banks he used to stash his drug money throughout the country. As it turned out, one of those banks was dangerously close to the apartment where I stayed for a few weeks at a time while running jobs in Colombia. When that bank was blown up, the floors of my apartment shook and the walls rocked. The noise was terrifying.

Follow the Oil

I made up my mind pretty quickly. There were plenty of other countries outside the borders of Colombia where I could catch jobs—and not risk getting blown up!

But like I said, this was one near miss where I came home with more than just a sigh of relief. You see, I just really liked the gold color of that house in Colombia. So today, my waterfront home in Corpus Christi, built in 2007, just happens to be gold colored. I always like to watch the reactions of people who visit me when I say, "Let me tell you the story of how I came to choose gold as the color for this house," and I explain all about Pablo Escobar and the pallets of $100 bills.

I could describe other wild and crazy times during my international travels in building up Magnum's business, but you know what? Even with all those very scary moments, I wouldn't trade that time and those experiences for anything. I got to work closely with oil giants like Amoco, Exxon, Mobil, and other major international companies. I learned so much more about how to identify, design, and utilize new tools and equipment that would support and enhance oil and gas operations. I met lots of great people, shook lots of hands, sampled food from many different countries and cultures, and saw some amazing sights. And I came home with all those foreign coins and the colorful stories I could tell about them.

I spent many weeks and months on the road during those years in the late 1980s and early '90s. All that time, I realized that I still had a business to watch over back home. Magnum kept up its strong presence in Oklahoma City, whether I was running things out of the Sea-Can and the garage turned into a shop at my home, or the office space I rented in a strip mall later. We continued to evolve, and that meant dealing with changes.

For one thing, I no longer used my *Magnum P.I.* connection when courting new customers. The TV show's popularity had faded, and my little red Ferrari cars got put on the shelf. At one point I decided to rebrand the main color of Magnum. Instead of red, our color was now John Deere green. Somebody who had been in the oil business for many years asked me why I didn't choose one of the more common colors for oilfield operation businesses, like yellow, red, or blue. Why green? I just smiled and said, "Because green is the color of money."

Another change, which I knew that I had to make after having some of my equipment copied, was to start seeking patents for my new tools and products. Over the course of several years, I would successfully register the amazing total of about 120 different patents.

Having patents didn't always prevent others from trying to put their name on my products, but it did cut way down on potential problems. It also contributed to our presence and credibility within the oil and gas industry. Those patents made a statement: We were riding the wave of new products and new technology, which meant that in the big, wide world of oilfield operations, we deserved to be taken seriously. And every once in a while, I would allow myself to sit back and say to myself, "More than one hundred patents? Not bad for a guy who draws his designs on a napkin."

As I look back over the first fifteen years of Magnum's history, while I was still living in Oklahoma, I remember that we also had to weather the dips and downturns in the oil industry. We took a few hits, like everybody else in the oil patch, but we didn't get hurt nearly as badly as other companies. I believe that's because our products and technology were new, and they worked extremely well. They would always be needed, until we came up with the next best thing.

Innovation, especially in my case, tends to have an interesting story behind it. When I was about ten years old, I was out gathering eggs in the chicken coop on our farm. As I was coming back to the house with a big basket of eggs, I saw my Dad standing outside on the porch. I asked him why the eggs sometimes got broken.

He said, "If we could train our chickens to lay their eggs upright there wouldn't be a problem."

"What do you mean Dad?" I replied.

He said, "Watch this, son," and picked up an egg from the basket,

Follow the Oil

laying it longways in my open hand. "Now squeeze this egg as hard as you can, with all of your might." He just stood there as I squeezed that egg with all my might . . . and nothing happened! It did not break; I couldn't believe it. I asked how that could happen. He explained to me that the egg's oblong shape was one of the strongest and is similar to the shape of arches used on bridge and building construction. I was amazed! He then took the egg and turned it sideways and placed it back in my hand. He asked me to squeeze it again as he stepped back. As I began squeezing down on the egg, it cracked open, and the contents splashed all over me and the porch we were standing on together.

Many years later, in 1994, I designed the MagnumDisk™ that utilized a ceramic rupture disk to hold back the oil or gas well. I recalled the lesson my Dad taught me about the egg and designed the disk to be shaped like the strongest portion of that egg. Later after we commercialized the product line, it needed a part number for our operations. After the shape and dimensions, I named it "CE-238" Chicken Egg, 2-3/8" O.D.

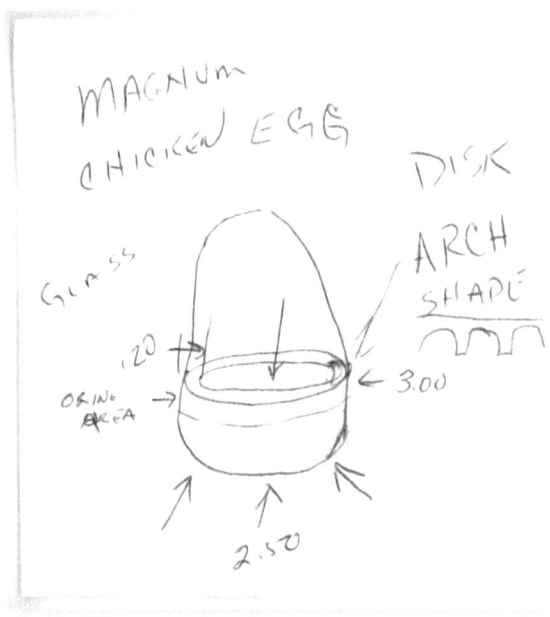

Also, I just continued to get better at talking with clients and listening to what they needed and then going back and trying to come up with some new and effective solution to their problems. This ability helped to steer one of my most popular mottoes that I would share with all my people at Magnum:

"Make your customer a hero."

How do you make your customers heroes? You provide them with something new and different, something that makes their operations hum more efficiently and effectively. They were heroes because they had found something to solve their problem, something that helped them shine and soar. And the more they soared, with our products and services helping to lift them higher, the more they would entrust in us to serve them over and over again. Why wouldn't you want to do business with some company that helped make you look like a hero?

I know that a big part of our success, beginning with those early years and continuing right up until we sold the business in October 2018, was that we were delivering something that our customers really, really needed to optimize their success in the oil and gas industry. And then, once they started using that tool or product that we provided, they learned that they could not do without it.

I faced many other changes and challenges during my first phase of running Magnum. Many of them were related to my business, but some changes were happening in my personal life too.

I decided at one point to try to learn to fly a small plane. I still had fond memories of flying with Uncle Anthony, Uncle Warren, and Uncle Ricky in their crop-dusting Piper Cubs, so when a doctor friend of mine told me he was interested in flying, he and I went in together on buying a 182 Cessna. I planned to earn my pilot's license, and after the first four-and-a-half hours of basic instruction, I was up there with my instructor, doing all kinds of maneuvers. I'd like to think I was doing pretty well at it, too, until it came time for a landing and I hit a strong crosswind.

My little Cessna was doing some serious yawing, its nose moving and dipping from side to side. When I finally got the plane down for the landing, we hit so hard I thought I was going to rip the wheels off. That was it for me as a pilot! I never even wanted to climb into a plane like that again. I still have the bag with all the VHS instructional tapes and books, though. Like I said, I'm a hoarder.

A more serious change in my personal life came along while Garrett and Derrick were still growing up. My marriage with my wife Cynthia wound up going through a long separation and eventually a divorce. There are usually many factors that can lead to a marriage not working out, and out of respect for the privacy of everyone involved, I will not go into all the details of the breakup of my first marriage. I will just acknowledge that my own actions were very, very wrong, and they strongly contributed to a long period of a very unsettled family life.

During that period, I was not able to spend nearly as much time as I would have liked to with my sons. I did get to coach Garrett and Derrick in many of their rec teams in baseball, football, and soccer when they were young. As they got older, I tried to make it to their ball games and show up for other events whenever I could. But with all the traveling required by my work running Magnum, along with restrictions from my marital separation agreement, I couldn't always be present where and how a boy should have his father present.

Little did I know back then that someday the three of us would have a chance to totally flip that picture. I could not predict that we would be able to closely share in something so big and so meaningful that would drive us to such a strong and meaningful relationship.

I had that hope, that dream, but I would discover that it was going to be a gradual process. It would happen step by step, with many twists and turns along the way.

CHAPTER 5

CORPUS CHRISTI CALLING

Looking back, I can honestly say that the occasion of moving from Oklahoma City to Corpus Christi in 2000 was a euphoric day for me. As it turned out, my (new) wife Trish, whom I married in 1994 after my divorce, and I would both fall in love with Corpus Christi.

Making this move was an exciting change even though I had to borrow off my MasterCard just to pay off my American Express bill to cover the expenses of hauling our family's belongings and my company's materials down to Texas. And even though the house and property that we bought in the Calallen suburb of Corpus Christi was going to take a lot of work. A *whole* lot of work! Also, I can say now that moving to Corpus really was a euphoric day despite the reality that I would need to quickly build up a bunch of new contacts and sales prospects to successfully operate Magnum in a different city and different state. It is important to mention that while we were committed to the new beginning, we still needed to maintain and service the valuable contracts and work back in Oklahoma.

So why was I so excited about rumbling nine hours down I-35 from Oklahoma City and starting over in a new location? For one thing, it wasn't really a new place to me. Corpus Christi was only eighty miles from my hometown of Port Lavaca. Our family didn't come to the big city of Corpus Christi much when I was a kid, but as a college student in Kingsville I would often drive there to check out the beaches and the night life, and to hang out with friends. I wasn't coming home exactly, but the Corpus Christi area of South Texas was very comfortable and familiar to me.

This move also brought me back to the water. My life had never been all that far from the Gulf Coast before I moved to Oklahoma, and although I did have Lake Hefner nearby for my sailboat adventures in Oklahoma City, I missed everything about being close to ocean waters. I wanted to smell the sea air again, and I always did have a special fondness for palm trees.

And all that work it was going to take to whip our new house and property into shape? To me, fixing up a new house is a lot like building a company. It was just something to sink my teeth into, a way to call upon my ability to envision something bigger and better, and then set about to make it happen. I liked starting out on a task and imagining that day when I could stop, take a look back, and say, "Wow, look what we created here!"

Even before renovations, this was a nicer house than the home we left in Oklahoma City. Situated on County Road 73, it was located in a real neighborhood. It had an in-ground pool out back, along with a large detached garage that would be perfect for setting up operations for Magnum. Our property had two and a half acres to work with. Oh, and Sam's BBQ was just down the street. It wasn't anything impressive, just a small trailer on the side of the road with a portable building constructed on it, with a screened-in porch. But the wonderful aroma of burning mesquite would lure us in to get dinner there once or twice a week.

It didn't take me long to start moving from vision to reality on the home front in Calallen. I cut twenty-one mesquite trees to clear space and planted palm trees and banana trees that my dad bought me. I built a deck around the pool and bought several palm trees from Walmart to place around there to make it look even nicer. Going further with my image of what could be, I put in a pond, complete with a fountain, and stocked it with fish.

Then came the really fun part: we added an outdoor bar and barbecue pit under a palapa roof. That backyard feature would soon become a popular hot spot for parties that my wife, Trish, and I hosted for adults, and as time went on both Garrett and Derrick got to throw big bashes that were a hit with all their friends.

After clearing out two-and-a-half acres around the house, Trish and I had to spend practically all day every Saturday just mowing. But even that felt worth the investment of time and energy. This was just where I knew I needed to be.

Anyway, I was never one who was afraid of making changes or heading off in a whole new direction in life. And in many ways, the time was ripe for a major change.

I was proud that I had leaped into the oil and gas industry right out of college and then carved out a place for my own business in a world that I had never expected to join. I had kept chugging along through the early struggles and had succeeded in making a living operating Magnum over those first fifteen years in Oklahoma. We had built on our bread-and-butter explosives work with the creation of the MagnumDisk™, the ceramic disk that acted as a frangible pressure barrier that had multiple applications in the well completion process. This product had been doing very well for us. We were paying our bills and making a little money here and there. But were we really growing anything substantial? Not really, at least not to the level that matched my dreams and visions for what could be. Now, with the move to Corpus Christi, I really believed that Magnum was primed for that next big step. If the words in my head at that time had been captured by some recording device, they probably would have sounded something like this:

"Now that I'm here, I know what I've got to do. I need to start coming up with new tools, new equipment, and new ideas to stay on top of or ahead of the market. I've got to knock on doors and make myself known. I've just got to rev up, retool, and find every way I can to start making Magnum really take off!"

As we forged ahead, Trish was instrumental on the administrative side of Magnum. I'll describe her contributions in more detail in a moment.

It was a natural time for new opportunities because the whole oil and gas industry was going through big changes. Fracking had already been making its mark in the 1990s and was becoming even more dominant as the new century began. Horizontal drilling and fracking opened huge doors for new oilfield locations across many different areas of the United States, which meant that companies like ours didn't have to focus nearly as much time and energy in far-off countries.

Fracking also changed how oilfield operations were designed and completed. The methods of running explosives into the wells had evolved while I was still in Oklahoma. It used to be that the oil company would run tubing into the vertical hole with Magnum's perforating guns on the bottom of the tubing string. With the change to horizontal drilling and fracking, we were still running guns on tubing in the toe of the horizontal well, but the remainder of the well had to be perforated via electric wireline and pumped to the depth before the internal casing could be perforated.

I had always aimed to stay flexible, so we were able to keep up with those new methods. But it was clear that new changes would continue to come along in the industry. A company like ours would have to stay on top of all those changes and anticipate the new products and services that would make those oil companies' operations as smooth and productive as possible. Staying "flexible" or adaptable to changes was important because it would mean you were accepting your current conditions and saying to yourself right now is "good enough" but it is not the end; it's merely a milestone in this long journey called life.

As I strategized about how to attract new customers and opportunities, we had a fun idea: pool parties. I'd throw a party and invite a bunch of my new neighbors and friends, but I would also be sure to include some local contacts from the oil and gas industry.

"Why don't you come over for a beer?" I would say to them.

When these oil industry guys came, Trish and I made sure they had a great time hanging out with everybody else by the pool and barbecue pit, talking shop. Amid all the fun and free-flowing banter, I always managed to find a few minutes to pick their brains and gather more info about what was needed in their work right then. After a while, those oil guys were enjoying hanging out at my backyard pool and barbecue pit so much they didn't even wait to be invited. They just started dropping by.

This was another example of how I always tried to think outside the box. I knew that it wasn't going to work so well just to ask industry contacts to visit me in my office, when that "office" was a garage space in back of my house. A couple of times I remember driving in my pickup and getting a call from some big-time player in our industry, and the person calling would suggest sending someone over to meet me at my office.

"Tell you what," I would say. "I'm on the road in my pickup right now. Why don't we figure out a good place to meet along the way?"

Fortunately, I outgrew my garage office within three years and rented an office space in a strip mall just around the corner from my house. I was already beginning to make things happen in South Texas when I came up with an idea for a new frac plug.

As usual, it began with one of my simple drawings. This composite frac plug was different from most of the plugs used in fracking at that time because the others were made entirely of fiberglass and mine was made of phenolic laminate material that was easier to mill up. This economic, lightweight material was similar to a strong, cotton-like material, almost like T-shirt material that is reinforced with epoxy like a roll of paper towels. There were also a few aluminum components to add strength since composites tended to fail under the pressures.

After sourcing the material and marketing the new frac plug, the MILL-EZ™, I soon discovered that it was only going to cost me about $1,000 to make a plug. With horizontal drilling and fracking we could sell each one for about $6,000. That was crazy money for Magnum back then!

So, things were beginning to move forward, just as I had been envisioning. But there was that one other change that had always been a part of my dreams for the future. I wanted Magnum to be a real family business.

My wife Trish was already a part of our operation when we moved to Texas. Back in Oklahoma, Trish had run a successful answering service business that I had set up for her. At one point, it had become the largest answering service business in the state, with twenty-six people screening calls for an assortment of doctors, lawyers, realtors, and other professionals. After a while, Trish joined me in helping to run Magnum. She handled all the accounting so I could focus on the design, mechanical, and day-to-day operational side of the business, and her strong organizational skills were a boost to our administrative side.

Now I just needed to complete my vision by bringing my two sons into the Magnum orbit. That desire to have my boys with me had become stronger after we moved to Corpus Christi. The boys were getting older, and I could sense that Magnum was going to really start taking off.

The way I looked at it, every father has the responsibility to take care of his kids. My hope was that the three of us could work together in a highly successful manner so that Garrett and Derrick could look back and say to themselves, "I could do that!" And then, when I reached the point where I wanted to retire, they could continue to grow Magnum even bigger than I had dreamed.

As I mentioned earlier, bringing my sons on board the Magnum train was a step-by-step process. Both Garrett and Derrick had to find their own way toward making the commitment to join me in our business, and it didn't happen overnight. Each one had his own strengths, and it was up to me to find those strengths and strategically integrate them into Magnum's operation.

I could explain how that all worked out from my perspective, but I think it would be better if I let my boys tell it in their own words. So, in these next pages, Garrett and Derrick will head back in time to share what it was like to grow up with my business in the house, and then they will go on to talk about how they followed the other important steps along the path that eventually led them to take their own place in Magnum.

Since Garrett is the oldest, he'll go first:

Garrett's Story

The first person we, as men, naturally look up to in life is our fathers. From the moment we speak our first word, shortly followed by our first steps, we are watching and parroting their actions, words, and expressions. I believe each little boy in his heart wants to grow up to be "just like dad."

And, from my earliest years, that's what I recall—watching, absorbing, and making decisions based on the actions and lessons from my father.

I was only four years old when Dad launched Magnum in Oklahoma. I remember riding in his pickup to the machine shop, picking up equipment, and heading on to jobs at the well site. Years later, taking your kids to a well site would be considered a no-no, of course, but nobody complained about it back then. While my dad handled his business, I would entertain myself back in the truck, or the lobby of a high-rise, quietly playing with my green U.S. Army men or coloring in my coloring book.

At home, I would watch my dad sitting at the kitchen table drawing his designs at his drafting table, with his T-square, mechanical pencil, and grid paper by his side. I have vivid images of looking at his briefcase, with its little gold combination flip locks, and saying to myself, "I want a briefcase like that someday."

During my youth, my parents were also running their screen-printing T-shirt business. Eventually, Dad showed Derrick and me how to tie-dye shirts. We would set up our folding table on the street corner and sell the T-shirts to neighbors and passers-by. Sometimes Dad let me take some of the reject shirts and sell them to the kids at school.

We were encouraged to try other little businesses. Like many kids, we had a lemonade stand for a while. My dad also showed us how to put up a little sign that says, "Free Car Wash," with the idea that people who let us wash their cars would give us a good tip when we were done. That plan was working okay until I washed my friend Steven's dad's car. After I spent what seemed like an hour getting that Buick all clean and shiny, Steven's dad drove away with a little wave goodbye—no tip! I learned my lesson: If you don't set your price for what you're selling, you risk getting nothing at all.

Another little side hustle was carried out during Christmastime. When the leaves would fall out of the trees in early winter in Oklahoma, mistletoe would be left behind on the otherwise empty tree branch. I would notice those mistletoes on the trees by the creek near our house while my friends and I were fishing, building tree forts, and re-creating our own real-life *Lord of the Flies*. My dad had an idea about this. One day he took us out into the country with a ladder, a long pole, and a little saw. He filled the whole back of the truck with mistletoes he cut off the trees. When we got home, my mother helped us prune the little bits of mistletoe and tie a ribbon on each one, with a little curly Q. We filled up our red wagons with these fancy mistletoes, and, a few weeks before Christmas, we'd go door to door selling them.

I have fond memories of my dad encouraging my genuine efforts to earn a dollar, and I appreciated his direction and can-do attitude. But, I have to admit, I did not grow up dreaming about the day I could go to work with him at Magnum. In fact, there were many times as a boy when I would say to myself, "I'm NEVER going to work in the oil and gas industry!" Growing up, my dad had to travel a great deal in pursuit of his ambitions. Therefore, I concluded this: If you worked in oil and gas, you'd always be away from your family. I held on to that belief even into my teenage years, at the time when my parents were going through a separation and divorce. I was upset with my parents, and the world, for the unfairness of it all. Add a healthy dose of teen hormones, and a young man can get pretty rebellious when left to his own devices. More times than I care to admit, when push came to shove, it leaked out sideways in the form of anger, aggression, and a steely resolve. So that promise I made to myself that "I'm never going to work in the oil and gas industry" just got stronger and stronger.

Despite all this, inside I was still just a boy who admired and sought approval from his father in any way possible. I even decided to use his number on my football jersey: 45. He came to a fair share of my games, but if I'm honest, the majority of the memories that I have are me wishing he was there to celebrate my wins and support me in the struggles. But the reality was that when forced to decide between parents as a fourteen-year-old, I chose to live with my mother. And the consequence of that was a strained relationship with my father. Although we lived in the same city, outside of the arranged custody visits, we didn't see much of each other during those years. And as young boys do, to cope with the absence of a father figure, I found acceptance and camaraderie among a small group of friends and sports teams—friendships that are still intact to this day, twenty-five years later. Many of those friends also had gone through a divorce, so there was a common bond between us. There I found an identity: the "tough guy" and protector. That role often led to rowdy behavior and fights against opposing teams and social circles. But that was my crew, and back then I didn't understand that the persona I was developing was a shield I put in place to mask feelings of rejection and to compensate for the lack of stability and guidance I so desperately desired.

I was living with my mother when I graduated from high school, and the only thing I knew for sure about college was that I wanted to keep playing sports. After taking a road trip with Dad to visit some potential colleges to play football or soccer, I wound up at Richland College, a two-year school in Dallas where I made the soccer team as a goalie. Early in the season, we were playing on the road against the defending national champions led by a Jamaican player who happened to be doing a lot of trash-talking during the game. After two halves of listening to it, he was firmly under my skin. When the game went into the second overtime, the other team scored the winning goal on me. On my knees, with my head down and feeling the hurt of defeat, I was in no mood to be messed with when he approached me gloating and hurling insults. Those feelings I always tried so hard to bury came rushing to the surface. All I saw was red, and the next thing I knew he was lying face down on the turf, while I stood over him clutching a crushed right hand. There went my season.

Believe it or not, there was a positive that came out of this experience. While driving nine hours back from that game, with no pain medication, and then later while working on my recovery, I began reflecting on my problem. I realized that for far too long, I had been letting my emotions get out of control, and the price I paid kept rising. Breaking my hand that day cost me the season, but it gifted me the rare opportunity of total self-awareness. From then on, I worked extremely hard to develop a calm steadiness and self-control, and it wasn't easy. I came back the next season and helped lead our team to a 13–3 record.

When my time at Richland came to a close, I decided to move back home to Oklahoma City. In a crazy turn of events, my girlfriend Trish (who is now my wife) somehow convinced me to enroll at Rose State College on scholarship as a male cheerleader on her co-ed team. Although I didn't initially take it seriously, we ended up going to nationals in Vegas and had a blast. From there I thought I might go on to Oklahoma State and pursue a degree in landscape architecture. At the same time, I was putting together a highlight video to send to college soccer coaches. The truth was, I really didn't know what I wanted to do with my life. And, when I temporarily broke up with Trish, I felt even more lost.

It was approaching the summer of 2001. My dad and Derrick were already living in Corpus Christi at that time. Since I hadn't seen my brother in a long time and only talked to my dad occasionally on the phone, I decided to come down to hang out for a couple of weeks. Little did I know that spur-of-the-moment visit would open the door to a whole new direction for me academically, professionally, and personally. And it was a direction I had once promised myself I would never take.

As my dad and I started catching up on lost time, and I let him know that my plans were pretty much up in the air, he encouraged me to consider Texas A&M University–Corpus Christi. I agreed to visit the campus, and I had to admit that the pristine view of the bay and the palm tree–lined pathways did look appealing. The big sell for Corpus didn't end there. He also dangled something else to consider for the future: joining him in the operation of Magnum Oil Tools and make good on the promise that he would pay for my degree.

I had come to a crossroads, and now I was forced to revisit the motives behind that vow I had made to myself as a kid. I was older now, and I realized it wasn't so much about choosing to work in this particular industry; it was more about choosing to work with my dad. Deep down, that heart of a child was still seeking the approval of his father, and to build a strong and close relationship with him. This was our chance to repatch those lost years. And on top of that, I could see the beginnings of a secure path for my future. The more I thought about it, my hardline position began to melt away.

Dad had a specific idea for how I could best contribute to Magnum's growth. "You're a natural-born salesman, Garrett—you could sell blisters to a track team," he would say. "And I need someone who can really boost our marketing and sales efforts, play golf, and drink beer!" I transferred to Texas A&M–Corpus Christi for that fall semester and steered my academic path toward a business degree with an emphasis in marketing.

Along the way, I began working part-time for Magnum, learning the business from the ground up. Dad had posted a sign above the workbench: "There's a place for everything and everything should be in its place." Before starting any procedure at Magnum, Dad taught me to begin with a clean, uncluttered workspace. My number one priority to begin each day was to sweep and organize the shop, and my number one priority at the end of the workday was to sweep up the shop again and return everything to where it belonged (my wife is most likely experiencing extreme outrage upon learning this).

All the products that Magnum sold at that time needed to be cleaned and assembled according to Dad's procedure, which meant picking up the manufactured parts from the machine shop and cleaning and stocking the engineered components to be ready for assembly. Then, when an order came in from one of our customers, we would hand-write the ticket, build the order, box it up, put the shipping label on it, and place it by the front door for FedEx to pick up.

For our local customers, my dad gave me a pair of coveralls and a pair of steel-toed boots to wear for in-person deliveries. When I would make the delivery, I would wait to make sure that the item was exactly what the customer ordered. Soon I began stopping by their offices first thing in the morning, just to drop off breakfast tacos as a little gesture of appreciation on my way to class. Before leaving, I would casually inquire whether there was anything that we could get for them that day. I guess you could say that was the start of my sales role with my dad's company.

Meanwhile, I was taking my time to complete my studies at college. Trish and I had gotten back together, and since she was now attending Texas A&M–Corpus Christi herself, we coordinated our schedules to graduate together in spring 2004. Due to my own scheduling mistake, however, I was not able to take my capstone course during that last semester and had to take it that summer, which put me in a predicament trying to balance both school and work.

By that time, I was doing more and more at Magnum, and business was booming. I was not only taking orders for our products and assembling those products; I also had begun to go out on jobs to run our products in the wells for some of the South Texas oil and gas companies. When I had to miss a presentation prep meeting at school because I was out on one of those jobs, I wound up getting a shaky review from some of my peers. I visited Dr. Middleton, professor of strategic management, and tried to explain how I had only missed the class because I was helping my father during a critical time with his business.

"Frankly, Garrett," she said before I went any further, "I don't think you have what it takes to be a successful strategic management professional."

You can bet those words stuck with me. After completing my degree, getting only a C for that capstone class, I took some time off to travel and then set my course to go full speed ahead with Magnum. With that same steely resolve, I knew someday I was going to prove that professor wrong. And, at just thirty-eight years of age, after I had developed and led a sales and marketing effort that helped us grow into a company worth half a billion dollars, I'd say that's just what I did.

Derrick's Story

While I was growing up, I was drawn to the cultural image of how a family should live: dad and mom together at home, white picket fence outside, the family sitting down together for dinner every evening at six o'clock, things staying consistent like that, year after year. I guess I had a tendency to want what I didn't have.

From early on in my childhood, however, I could see that it was never going to be like that in our family. I was only a year old when my dad launched Magnum, so all my early memories were of those days when he was traveling for work for long periods of time. He just always seemed to be working in some far-off land. For years, I didn't even know what he was doing in his work. I just couldn't fully appreciate what he was doing or sacrificing; I was too young.

I was still in elementary school when my parents separated. This time in Garrett's and my life really made us grow up fast, way too fast for kids. At first, I felt more comfortable living with my mom, just because she was around more and seemed more reliable. My mom loved my brother and me, and she would do anything for us: She worked long hours at her T-shirt screen-printing business, just to make ends meet and to ensure that we kept up with the latest trends to look "cool" like our friends.

However, those long hours she kept in an effort to provide more for us meant that she was not able to be around after school. This left my brother and me home alone after school, when we would get into all sorts of trouble. Fights with each other and with the neighborhood kids were common. After watching the example of a couple of my friends and taking in what TV had taught me about what a conventional family looked like—a father and mother at the dinner table with loving siblings around—I began to desire that. Years later, as my dad began to travel less, he continued to work out of the house while living with his girlfriend at the time. From my perspective, I guess this seemed like an opportunity for me to have a piece of that cultural norm I desired: a child's image of how family life was supposed to be.

It was a pivotal time in my life when, at age twelve, I broke the news to my mom that I wanted to spend more time with my dad and was going to go live with him and my future stepmom, to maybe get a piece of that "cultural norm." So it was arranged for me to live with him. To this day, I still look at this event as one of the most difficult days in my childhood. I had knots in my stomach as I told my mom, who loved me so dearly, that I was choosing my dad over her. I felt horrible, stricken with pain and guilt after making a decision no child should face, let alone make, and certainly no mother should hear from her own son.

After the dust had settled and things began to normalize, while I was going to Hefner Middle School in Oklahoma City, my dad and soon-to-be stepmom started to give me chores: how to clean up my penmanship, how to take notes during class, how to keep a daily task journal, as well as tasks to help him with Magnum. As I look back, I realize this guidance provided me a sense of security and structure that wasn't available at my mom's house with my older brother.

I can remember when he would pay me $10 for every tool I would assemble. I was very practical about my financial needs, so if I needed to make $50 for something I wanted to buy, I would stop my assembly process when I finished five tools. From my perspective, that made perfect sense. The only problem was that my dad had specifically told me that I had to complete ten of those tools to finish the job. I learned about doing what one was expected to do . . . slowly. This opportunity to have a little money, along with some security, provided me with a safe mental place and began building a structure for success.

When Dad and my stepmom Trish moved down to Corpus Christi, I decided to go with them. That meant making the adjustment to a new school, Calallen High School, during my sophomore year. With Dad working out of the garage at home, I was around his business regularly and continued to help when I had time.

This was another time when I felt I had let my mom down—when I had to break the bad news to her that I was moving from Oklahoma City to Corpus Christi with my dad and stepmom.

My mom was incredibly supportive and extremely involved in my brother's life during high school, supporting him every way she could, at pep rallies, student leadership events, and with his friends. She was like a mom to the whole crew, my brother's crew that is. And when I told her I would be moving to Corpus, I can only imagine how disappointed she must have been to hear that she would not be a part of my high school years, disappointed to be robbed of the opportunity to be involved in my high school life. But despite the nine-to-ten-hour drive down I-35 from Oklahoma City to Corpus, she still found ways to show up for me. She was determined to continue to love and support me no matter what. I was thankful and extremely proud when she was in the stands cheering me on at football games.

At that time, during high school, I have to admit that I just did not see any picture of my future that had Magnum in the center of it. I was too young at the time; my only thought was that this was my opportunity to move to another city, to get out of my brother's shadow as "Lil Frazier," and start anew with the hopes of continuing in my father's footsteps through my dream of playing college football at a Division I school.

Magnum at that time was still a relatively small company. My dad was running things out of the garage until he moved to an office in a strip mall and then to larger offices later. As an adolescent and later as a young adult, I envisioned myself and my future as a part of something much bigger. I didn't know what kind of company I wanted to work for, but I imagined that it would be in some city that was larger than Corpus Christi, someplace that had more of a metropolitan feel. People would sometimes speak for me by saying things like, "I could definitely see you in California."

My vision of professional life also did not fit the image I had of working in the oil and gas industry. Back then, I had a preconceived negative notion and some actual interactions with people from oil and gas that made me believe it was just a gritty industry populated by a bunch of roughnecks. That wasn't for me. I was going to do something different.

As I considered my options for college, I knew that I wanted to study economics or finance. I imagined myself doing work where I would look super professional and speak in a very polished manner. That was a lot different from how my dad came across in his role of leading Magnum. With his down-to-earth talk and his untucked shirts, you wouldn't exactly say he looked 100 percent polished. He was genuine, 100 percent genuine, and real salt of the earth. Just maybe not what I had envisioned myself becoming.

Also, when I graduated from high school in Corpus Christi, I still considered Oklahoma, not Texas, as my home. That was a major reason I chose the University of Oklahoma (OU), which was only a half hour from Oklahoma City where I had grown up and my mother still lived.

While studying economics at OU, I took a semester off to experience life at an Outward Bound school in Costa Rica. I enjoyed the surfing and whitewater rafting and learning more about the conservation of forests and oceans, which was something I already had been interested in. Getting involved in those kinds of causes just seemed to be pulling me further and further from oil and gas, which to me represented the opposite from this new world. For people in these environmental arenas, oil and gas was not exactly looked upon in the most positive light.

Costa Rica Outward Bound gave me a lot, including my love for the ocean and a sense of purpose. But, more than anything, it provided me my relationship with Jesus Christ. At OU, I had been struggling with an "existential crisis." Even though I was surrounded by incredible friends and a loving girlfriend, I wasn't happy. I couldn't knock that feeling. I tried hard to "get happy," but I just couldn't shake the loneliness and feelings of always desiring to be somewhere or something else. I concluded that I needed to leave all of that struggle behind and go somewhere to figure out what was going on inside of myself. During this time, I had begun to reach out to my brother, I guess searching for help from a loved one, someone I trusted. This trip was a transformational experience for me on so many levels. After I up and left Norman and "dumped" all of those who loved me (Ryan, Harrison, Blake, Dusty, and Chris, to name a few), I was lonely, extremely lonely. Not only was I in the middle of a rain forest in Costa Rica with no sight or feeling of home nearby, but I was also left with just a few pieces of literature from back home. Specifically, I had a book my brother had given me on the trip, *Dinner with a Perfect Stranger* by David Gregory (2005). This book, while simple and short, was a vital tool for me. I was deeply drawn in by quotes like this:

> *"There's no adventure like being joined to the Creator of the universe. . . . And your first mission would be to let him guide you out of the mess you're in."*

Soon I found myself in a river of the Monte Verde Mountain during a tree-dwelling shaman's cleansing ritual of the mind, body, and soul. Internally, I had no clue what was going on, why I was there, or what had brought me to that moment in time. The ritual consisted of silently crawling into a rock-formed, grotto-like sauna with heated rocks in the center for ten minutes and then cleansing yourself in the river, a process to be repeated three times.

Leaving everything I had and coming to a strange land in the middle of a rain forest was exactly what I needed to show me that if I was not accepting, loving, and happy with myself and others, I would never be able to fully appreciate the loved ones around me. So as a result, there in that river, in what seemed like a world away from everything I knew and loved, I accepted Christ.

I would still work for my dad during the summer months, and by that time Garrett had come to work for Magnum in Corpus. Slowly, my perceptions began to change. While doing everything from painting the floors to sitting in on sales presentations, I began to see the people there outside of the box I had placed them in. I admired the way that my dad could move gracefully among different groups of people, showing a genuine interest and a real caring for everyone, no matter what role they played or where they came from. Furthermore, I saw the way he would command respect and admiration through his leadership style and his knack for business.

Meanwhile, things were not going as well as I had been hoping at OU. I broke up with my girlfriend Ryan (who is now my wife; God love her, I put her through so much, and she has made me the man I am today) for a while, and I was again beginning to feel kind of lonely and curious about what the future would hold for me. Around that time, Garrett and I had begun to keep up regular communication. One day Garrett said something that opened my eyes about making a change I never expected to even consider.

"Hey, man," Garrett said, "we're building something really cool down here. We're really doing well with Magnum, and it looks like it's going to keep getting better and better. Maybe you could come here and join us, just be a part of something special."

I listened to what he was saying, gave it some thought, talked with my dad about it, and thought about it a lot more. Then, in August 2007, I took the big leap. I transferred to Texas A&M–Corpus Christi, just as Garrett had done a few years earlier, and I began to work at Magnum part-time while pursuing my degree. A little more than a year later, as fast as I possibly could, I graduated from Texas A&M–Corpus Christi and took a full-time job with Magnum, joining my dad and my brother in a formidable journey of a lifetime.

Taking these steps was a real gut-check for me. It meant putting aside what I thought was going to be my trajectory of plans: graduating from a Tier-1 university, going to work as a savvy professional in the financial sector, and moving to a larger metropolitan area, someplace even farther from home.

Instead, I was making a commitment to join a smaller company in a smaller city that was not far down the road from where my dad grew up. And rather than going off and making a name for myself on my own, I would be spending every workday around my father and my brother.

That last part was especially ironic because for much of my childhood in Oklahoma, people saw me as Garrett's little brother. In Oklahoma City, around school and on the athletic fields, they called me "Lil Frazier." That was one of the reasons that I decided to make the move from Oklahoma City to Corpus Christi to live with my dad and my stepmom while I was still in high school. I liked the idea of coming down to a totally new school and a life that was my own. While Garrett was off going to college in Dallas, I had a chance to get out from underneath his shadow and just maybe make a name for myself.

But it's interesting how life goes sometimes. A couple of years later, Garrett was moving to Corpus Christi to finish school and start work at Magnum. Now, here I was doing the very same thing.

And yet, I would come to learn this would be a pivotal building block for me. I would never have been able to know it at the time, but looking back, I am extremely thankful and at peace with the choices I made. I can see now that this was the right choice for me to make, because it was my path. Maybe not exactly as I would have planned it, but it was "my path" and I am at peace and forever thankful for it.

CHAPTER 6

THE TIES THAT BIND

Have you ever heard the term "perfect storm"? It became popular about twenty years ago after the successful movie *The Perfect Storm* came out, with its dramatic story of a commercial fishing boat that got caught in a rare combination of weather conditions that claimed the lives of the entire crew. Today, the term is sometimes used to describe any combination of circumstances that drastically aggravates some event or situation.

Usually, a perfect storm describes something negative. But since I always try to see things in a different light when it makes sense to me to do so, I think a perfect storm also can be used to describe something in a positive light. It can capture what happens when the perfect combination of people and abilities come together to create a force that's much bigger and more powerful than what only one person could achieve.

That's why I look at what happened in the years after my sons, Garrett and Derrick, joined Trish and me at Magnum as "a perfect storm." It just seems to fit our blending of different people, different sets of skills and abilities, different personalities, and different ways of looking at the world, all bonded by family ties and all committed to making Magnum grow and flourish.

As Garrett and Derrick learned the ropes and their roles in our company, we just came together in a natural and complementary way. I was designing the equipment and keeping a rudder on the ship. Garrett was out there in the waters creatively marketing and selling our products and services. And Derrick was pulling together the research and contacts to find the best way for our products to be built with the right people on board with us.

That's how our sturdy ship just kept sailing further and further, taking us beyond new horizons into clear, beautiful waters. And as we kept seeing over and over again, it's not the direction of the wind, but how you adjust your sails.

Any way you want to define it, we three Fraziers were definitely stronger together. I was the creative visionary, with the design ideas and the image of where we could go as a company. Garrett was the social guy, tapping and perfecting his natural marketing and sales skills. Derrick was the tightly focused one, studying the fine details of who and what could enable us to build and sell at a high level. We would just feed off one another. Design the product, get the manufacturers together, build the products, go out and sell them—boom, boom, boom!

This was how I had always hoped things would come together for us. I wanted Garrett and Derrick to come in, establish a foothold in the company, fall in love with what we were doing, and become major contributors and leaders of Magnum in their own right. As I would playfully tell people around me, I wouldn't trade Garrett and Derrick for anyone!

It was very gratifying for me to see how well it worked out. We faced the challenges of the downturns head-on and capitalized on the surges of growth and success we rode in those years leading up to the sale of Magnum, which totally fulfilled my dreams and visions.

When I think back to when it all first started to come about, I also have to say that it was an enormous relief for me. Before the boys entered the picture and took on their roles, I would describe my time at Magnum as "no rest for the wicked." As I described earlier, I was out there every day designing the products, assembling the products, selling the products, overseeing the use of our equipment on-site, cultivating business contacts, planning and managing our company's growth, and weathering all the little storms that came along. Trish handled the paperwork side of those endless days.

I always felt like I just couldn't afford to overlook anything that needed to be done. I did have helpers taking on various tasks and responsibilities, and many of them became invaluable to our operation. But I couldn't shake loose of the feeling that, minute by minute, I just had to be taking care of everything. Bringing the boys into the business started to change all that for the better.

Little by little, I could allow Garrett and Derrick to take on some of those responsibilities. I knew that I could rely on them to handle what I gave them, and that our family relationships would steer our communication in a way that we could build a stronger and stronger foundation of trust and effectiveness.

As we explored in the last chapter, moving to Corpus Christi marked the start of a major growth spurt for Magnum. It didn't take us long to outgrow our operation out of the garage that I had fixed up behind our home in Calallen and move into an 1,800-square-foot office in a strip mall.

After we moved into the strip mall, Brandon Munoz (Trish's youngest son) moved down to Corpus Christi to work at Magnum. I felt bad that none of her children had chosen to move with her. As a result, it felt right that we offered Brandon a job in assembly. He accepted the job and moved with his family. After a few years, he naturally excelled in a sales role for the western district of the United States.

This period was also a time when our father-son bonds were growing and changing. When Garrett made the decision to move to Texas and attend college in Corpus Christi while working for Magnum part-time, Derrick was already living in our house. To give Garrett his own space, I set up a 12 × 30 Morgan building out back, not far from the pond I put in. Garrett slept in this private structure but would join us in our house for dinner. The three of us had begun to spend more time together, even before we all joined hands in the operation of Magnum.

By the time Derrick transferred from the University of Oklahoma to finish school at Texas A&M–Corpus Christi and eventually come into the Magnum fold with us, we had already outgrown that strip mall office. I had moved the business into a 6,000-square-foot space in an undeveloped area of Corpus Christi on Southern Minerals Road. That location was perfect for a company like Magnum because we were almost surrounded by customers and competitors within our industry. I no longer had to feel insecure about inviting any new contact to come over to meet me in my office.

The Magnum story would not be complete without taking a moment to mention my good friend Ron Abt. Ron and I worked together while I was in a consulting role with Prime Perforating in Canada. He was a very smart, hard-working individual and I wanted to hire him shortly after we moved into the strip mall on County Road 624. At that time, Ron was working overseas in Saudi Arabia with another company. I asked him if he would come to work for us, but he told me that he and his wife, Yelena, were very happy where they were. A few months later that area of Saudi came under attack by terrorists. For several days during the attack Ron and his wife were separated with no way to communicate. He called, told me his story, and said he was ready to move to Corpus Christi and hire on. To which I replied, "great! Come on down!" Ever since then, Ron and his family have been a large part of Magnum and our family. He was indispensable in his role at Magnum; he brought structure and experience to the team. He focused on our operations at first, but in the end found his natural rhythm in international sales.

Later, for the final ten-year stretch of Magnum growth before the sale of our company, we bought a sprawling five-acre, 42,000-square-foot facility on Bear Lane. The place was so big that we initially sublet sections of it to two other companies. Four years later, we had terminated those leasing agreements and expanded to close to 100,000 square feet. That's how big Magnum was growing!

There's a lot more I could say about the growth and expansion phase of Magnum, and the big-time success we achieved during that time when the three Fraziers set sail together. But, just as my sons were major contributors in making it all happen, I think it's very fitting for them to describe their experiences during those years in their own words. They are the best sources to bring in the highlights of their specific contributions and how it all came together.

So, allow me to take a break while I invite my two sons back on stage.

Garrett's Reflections

Lynn would often say that he didn't end up doing the kind of work that he went to college to learn, which is common for many people today. In my case, however, with a bit of direction from Lynn, I stepped into Magnum doing exactly what I had learned in college.

While I studied marketing at Texas A&M–Corpus Christi, my courses included website development and graphic design. So, it was fitting that when I graduated and began working full-time at Magnum, one of my primary goals was to make sure that we had a clear, informative, up-to-date website to successfully market our products and services.

I developed a format for technical data sheets on each of our products that presented an easy-to-understand description of how each product worked and its many different specifications. I put in written form the assembly procedures, installation procedures, and running procedures for all of Magnum's tools so that when customers went online to assess our products, they would be looking at a detailed and professional presentation.

If our customers had questions, I wanted to give them answers. One way or another, my goal was to make them feel that Magnum would be their best home for the products and services they needed in all their well completion operations.

Before I settled into my position as Magnum's director of marketing and sales, it helped that I had already learned the company from the ground up from my part-time work and a brief initial stint as assembly coordinator. It was serendipitous that right around the time I went full-time, a major change in the oilfield drilling operations of an important customer spurred another round of rapid growth for Magnum.

Lynn began bringing me with him to participate in high-level sales presentations. One of the earliest experiences that I recall involved our work with EOG Resources, one of our customers in South Texas. They were paying a very high-dollar amount for a major competitor's composite plug. The area of Texas that EOG was drilling in was extremely hot, with extremely high pressures, and they began having some problems. They wanted a better way to isolate their hydrocarbon zones of interest and eliminate the problematic composite plugs. Lynn just did what he always seemed to be able to do when faced with this kind of challenge—he came up with a design for something that would fulfill the needs of our customer. His solution not only allowed EOG to isolate under high pressure and high temperature conditions, but also saved money by running this tool in the casing string. It simplified their operation by eliminating a wireline and coil-tubing runs. We ultimately called this new tool the Magnum Stimulation Valve.

After carefully checking out this product, EOG decided to run it. They were so impressed with the tool that they wanted to completely commercialize it, but Magnum at that time lacked the service capabilities and personnel to handle all the needed work for a change of that scale.

EOG had been getting its plugs and services from Halliburton then, so the opportunity before us was to sell our new product to Halliburton, which in turn would provide the service for EOG. Lynn and I flew off to meet with Halliburton at their fancy corporate office in a big, impressive high rise in Dallas. We were seeking to negotiate a major deal with one of the biggest players in oil and gas in the world.

Before we walked into that meeting, Lynn and I had carefully strategized how many of these tools we wanted Halliburton to commit to purchasing, and at what price. We knew the price that we would present to them, while keeping to ourselves the price that we would settle at.

We boldly and confidently pitched our price, and, sure enough, we struck exactly the deal that we wanted. Walking out of that high-rise that day, I felt like a champion. Lynn and I were still giving each other high fives when our plane touched down in Corpus Christi.

This was my first taste of big corporate negotiations, and I wanted to taste more. I wanted to do big deals, to find myself in the middle of high-pressure situations. What we did in that big high-rise that day is what I envisioned doing over and over, and on a bigger and bigger scale.

Yes, I was going to keep doing everything I could to successfully promote and sell our products and services, to become an important part of the face of Magnum. . . .

As time went on, we began to diversify our product portfolio, and our composite plugs were gaining traction and popularity in the oil patch. With vertical wells, a company would usually need to purchase three or four of our plugs per well. But when the Barnett Shale in Fort Worth kicked off horizontal drilling, they were suddenly requiring twelve to fifteen plugs per well. Seemingly overnight, our total market share grew exponentially. Instead of building ten to twenty plugs at a time for orders, we had to build hundreds.

To help keep up with this demand, I was taking orders over the phone, fulfilling those orders, delivering the plugs, and actually going out into the field and running the plugs in the wells. This experience definitely added to my confidence when writing about and talking about any part of our company's operation, to anyone, at any time, in any capacity.

While continuing to revamp our marketing communications, I also kept my eye out for potential upgrades in our sales techniques. With the continued expansion of fracking, Magnum was suddenly doing business in places like West Texas, Montana, Wyoming, West Virginia, and North Dakota. We were dealing with new customers in new territory, and I saw an opening to try something new in the face of our sales force. I had been down the road of hiring experienced men with established customer networks. So, in the oilfield world that had mostly been dominated by redneck-type guys, I wanted to try something different. I realized that our customer base was dominated by younger professionals who were impressionable and who liked to participate in social events and activities. So I decided to put like-minded people on the other end, matching what our customer base looked like. Additionally, I felt that women were much better with relationships, and in sales, it's all about the relationships. As a result, I began hiring women to handle our frontline sales efforts and business development functions.

Here's one example of how that turned out. We were able to attract some important business in the suddenly hot West Virginia region of the Marcellus Shale. I was told from the start that the people we'd be dealing with in this rural area of West Virginia were not rednecks; they were hillbillies. And there was a big difference.

One bumper sticker that seemed to keep showing up on the trucks around that area read, "TAFT." According to my contacts, that was an abbreviation for "This Ain't F— Texas!"

So you can imagine the initial shock when I assigned a woman to represent Magnum in our business in West Virginia. No one had ever entrusted women to serve as sales reps in such a blue-collar environment before. I was using a little psychology with this choice, counting on the surprise effect to work in our favor. And that's exactly what happened.

I hired more and more women to strengthen our sales efforts. As time went on, I noticed that some of our competitors were finally catching on and beginning to break down their own gender barriers.

The success of women in Magnum's sales positions went way beyond the initial surprise effect. From my experience, the reality is that women tend to build and maintain relationships easier and more effectively than men. When a woman sat down with a customer, that customer would really listen. Also, we offered a big carrot: a 1 percent commission on whatever they sold, and, in some cases, these ladies were selling millions of dollars of equipment per month. Other companies wouldn't do that, but we were happy when they made huge commissions because they were generating great business for us.

The women I hired also had the intelligence, ambition, and business skills to stand up in any presentation, no matter how male-dominated the audience might be, and they were consistently accountable. To be honest, guys who were knowledgeable about the industry and our products sometimes just didn't have strong enough people skills when it came to dealing with customers. And sometimes, when I gave a guy a specific assignment to be completed by a certain time, he would fall short of expectations and make excuses. Conversely, if I told one of the women on my team whom I had hired to do the same thing, she would get it done in twenty-four hours . . . no excuses.

Don't get me wrong; we had lots of terrific guys doing fantastic work for Magnum. But bringing in more women, in places where they had never been before, was just one more way to elevate our performance and cultivate the company and culture we desired.

As well as doing whatever I could to strengthen and enhance our day-to-day Marketing and Sales performance, I also welcomed the opportunity that Lynn provided me to get involved in the bigger picture of enhancing our position in the oil and gas industry. Lynn's original business plan back before Derrick and I came on board was brilliant—sell Magnum products to a company at one layer, and then that company would turn around and sell those products to bigger companies, taking a wholesaler position. What I came to find out after spending more time cultivating relationships with those service companies was that when they were presented with cheaper products, they were not loyal to Magnum. Therefore, the destiny of our company's future lay in the hands of companies that were not loyal to us because they were using our competitors' products to save a buck. I felt strongly that we had to do something about this because we found ourselves losing market share in several key areas. Against Lynn and Ron's wishes and opposed to how they were used to doing business, I persuaded them to let us sell direct to the oil and gas companies that were actually drilling and completing the wells, not just the service companies. This decision, although difficult, was a pivotal moment in our company's history because our customer base was no longer limited, and our profit margins increased substantially.

Derrick's Reflections

A phrase that continued to ring in my head that captured the perspective I carried with me in making the commitment to launch my business career with Lynn and Garrett at Magnum:

> "Trust that the path you are on has its purposes, and while on that path be passionate, courageous, and aware."

That attitude helped me see that even though I had not wanted to work in oil and gas when I was younger, the people I was dealing with, the opportunities that were presented to me, and the success that we had at Magnum all combined to bring out the best in me.

I have to admit, however, that I didn't come to that understanding right away. When I began in my first role as manager of inventory control in 2008, it happened to be around the time that the oil industry was taking a bit of a hit. That meant that one of my first tasks was to cut our inventory by about 30 percent.

I thought to myself, *Wait a second, this isn't how I thought it was going to be.* I figured I was coming in there to work with my dad and my brother and we'd do our work and just start cashing big checks and having fun. What was going on?

Fortunately, the oil bust did not hurt us nearly as badly as other companies due to our strategies and tight communication, and Magnum was soon back on the road to major growth. After a few years, I stepped into a new role as quality assurance manager. By then we were doing more of our business with bigger companies, and those companies were buying from us in larger volume. These companies needed to make sure that we had quality manuals in place, with a level of sophistication expected at that level. Within this role, I also began looking at the operations of our company and tried to introduce efficiencies where needed, to help ensure that the processes we followed were documented and that our people were consistently following those processes.

A critical role model and mentor for me and this process was Ron Abt. Ron had come to work at Magnum a few years before I joined the team full-time. He had a strong background with Baker Hughes and had a real vision and steadfast dedication to processes and quality. I will never forget Ron's six Ps: "Proper Preparation Prevents Piss Poor Performance." Ron was like a second father around the shop; he thrived off the institution of structure and order. Without him, we definitely would not have been as good as we were. He had a vast array of knowledge about quality assurance and operations, and for what he may have lacked in formal education on the subject, he made up for it with fortitude and drive.

Over time, my responsibilities evolved into serving as product manager. In this capacity, I found myself working with everybody from accounting to the design team, to sales, to the supply chain, to receiving, to assembly. I learned to become a bit of a chameleon in moving from conversation to conversation among these many different departments.

I also discovered more and more that my preconceived notions about the look and feel of life inside an oil and gas company just didn't match what I was seeing and experiencing every day. The folks I was around at Magnum weren't just a bunch of roughnecks at all. They were really great people with the necessary drive and unbridled support. I began to fully understand and appreciate that no matter where you were or what kind of industry you worked in, people are at the center of it.

Then, in the last few years before Magnum's sale to Nine Energy, I worked out a role for myself that would come to be called product development. Essentially, I was focused on how we would take our products from concept to commercialization. This is where I can say I really began to lean into my strengths with purpose and an identity. With the nature of the larger operation that we had at our company, there were many steps involved in moving from concept to the market and then being commercialized. But the company needed a leader and road map as we were getting bigger to continue to design customer-centered products and launch within a respective time frame. I was up for the challenge.

I created the MOPP—Magnum Optimal Product Process—as a guide for how we take a customer-centered designed product from concept to commercialization. During an initial discovery period, I would sit down with the various players in the company to gain a clear idea of what was essential and nonessential in developing a certain product. I would facilitate the research to help us identify the best materials to utilize in our product development, and I would go to trade shows to seek the right vendors, people whom we could trust to "get in the boat" with us so that we would all be rowing in the same direction, and who would support us and the product when problems occurred. I understood that as Magnum grew, it was becoming more and more important to cultivate relationships with vendors who were extremely supportive of Magnum and able to assist us in our growth.

I was also working with our designers or engineers to help them fully grasp exactly what was needed with a new product. Always keeping in mind Lynn's motto to "make your customer a hero," I would try to move us toward human-centered design products that our customers would want to buy and keep buying. In many ways, I was serving as a conduit between the customer and our design team. I would say to our designers, "Okay, guys, this is what's most important to this customer. Now let's sit down with them so you can ask them in more detail just what they're looking for." In my position, I kept encouraging us to keep our eyes open for anything that we could do, some little tweak to our product that might add even more value to our customer.

All along the way in this process, I would be consulting with Garrett to identify and provide everything that he and his team needed to go out there and successfully sell these new products. So, in that way, I was operating between two worlds: Lynn over here designing these products and setting the whole process in motion, and Garrett over there primed and ready to sell these products to some of the biggest companies in the world within our industry.

Another way that I worked in tandem with Lynn and Garrett was to add my perspective to our efforts to weave our culture into everything that we did. Magnum was no longer the kind of small company where you could just open your door and yell down the hall to somebody, "Hey, have you got me on that one?" By the time we were ready to sell the company, we had scaled to nearly 200 employees, with seven Magnum facilities in the United States and other strategic distribution points across the globe. From the beginning, Lynn had established a great culture at Magnum. With our expanded size came challenges to maintain the kind of core values and practices that we believed in.

During some renovations at the office, we had the opportunity to name our conference rooms: Trust Room, Expert Room, Simple Room, Driven Room, Innovation Room. The Driven Room seemed to fit a larger gathering when more technology-savvy matters would be discussed, while the Trust Room was more suitable for senior leadership meetings. I urged staff to use those names when scheduling meetings and to take them seriously, because I believe that words are important in setting a tone and direction to follow. If you're meeting in the Simple Room, for example, the idea is to treat questions and issues with a direct, simple approach, but if you found yourself in the Innovation Room, well, that was the time to be innovative in thought while designing equipment.

Since I was working with so many different people in various wings of Magnum's operation, I always tried to be aware of opportunities where I could facilitate positive change from within. For example, with my environmental views, I was certainly encouraged when we began to use recyclable packaging materials or reusable crates for repeat customers who desired to cut waste. I would advocate for using them more often and more consistently, even when they cost a little more.

Sometimes the difference I was seeking to make may have seemed small to other people, but when I believed it was important, I would fight for it. When I noticed how every single department in Magnum had its own Keurig single-serve coffee maker, I led the move toward using one centralized bean-to-cup coffee machine. Not only did this cut down on costs, but it also created an environment where people operating out of different silos or departments would start coming into more day-to-day contact with other staff members from different departments. That was helpful in maintaining our culture, and after a while those little grumblings and complaints about not having your own coffee maker, or watercooler, began to dissipate.

Sometimes I found myself going against the grain. That didn't usually bother me though, because I happen to feel comfortable with conversations in which different opinions and perspectives are tossed around. I strongly believe that there is always something important to be gained when two parties are willing to enter into those tough conversations. Even if Lynn might tell me, "You have your head in the sand," with some of my opinions about oil and gas and the environment, I appreciated that he was receptive to talking about it, to give each person the opportunity to speak their mind and air things out. I would always learn from those interactions.

I'm a person who is naturally passionate about my beliefs and perspectives, and I never wanted to get caught up in a routine where I was passionate about one issue in the office and passionate about another issue at home. Instead of an inner conflict, I sought to cultivate a greater ability to live in both worlds and to be at peace with each of them.

Thankfully, working with Lynn and Garrett and the other great people at Magnum, I found a way to do that. A way to be myself and be a part of something much bigger . . .

Making Up for Lost Time

So, that's a snapshot of how Garrett and Derrick looked at the picture of the perfect storm that I was talking about at the beginning of this chapter. Working in tandem, we pulled our abilities and efforts together with our people to bring Magnum to the pinnacle.

But I think there's more to this equation. "A perfect storm" also seems to perfectly describe how our relationships came together in new ways. As Magnum began to really soar, the ties that bind all fathers and sons just seemed to get stronger and stronger for us. And that was one more exciting part of our success!

I had always tried to keep up our father-son bonds, but during that unsettled period in our family in the midst of my separation and divorce with their mom, it wasn't always so easy. Facing a bunch of challenges, I did what I could to keep us connected. For example, I remember those Sundays Garrett and Derrick would spend with me while they were living with their mother, when the three "guys" would cuss and discuss what was going on in our lives. I also kept my eye out for the possibility of doing something a little different, something special together.

One year, I believe it was about the time when Garrett was starting college and Derrick was entering high school, I made a plan. "Guys, we're going to have a men's vacation," I told them. "We're going to Cancun, Mexico!" Working with a travel agent, I scored a great price for an all-inclusive excursion. I didn't pay much attention to what that travel agent said while she was showing me the photos of the place.

"As you can see, it's beautiful there," she said. "But you just need to know there are going to be a lot of differences: different languages and . . . other differences."

"No problem," I responded. "We're just going down there for the experience. We don't have many chances to do something like this with just the three of us."

So we traveled down there and checked in, and it really was beautiful. We scoped out the pool, and as I watched Garrett and Derrick talking to each other, I was saying to myself, "This is going to be great!" After a fantastic dinner, I said, "Okay, guys, we're going to get up early in the morning so we can come down here and eat breakfast. It's all-inclusive, you know. Everything is all paid for."

"Yeah, yeah," they muttered. But when I got up at 7:30 the next morning, took my shower, and said to my two sleeping sons, "Come on, time to get up, we're going to go eat breakfast now," they didn't budge an inch. It was probably 9:45 by the time I got them up. We were walking around the facility, and when we passed by the pool, we noticed a volleyball game going on. When we came a little closer, we noticed something else: The girls playing in that volleyball game were all topless!

Well, if that was the difference my travel agent was warning me about, she didn't have to worry about us. Apparently, the clientele at our resort included many French women and those from other countries where the idea of going around topless in public was just, well, natural.

The next day, I was still asleep; it was probably only 7 a.m., and the boys came and shook me awake. "Dad, come on, get up," they said, "let's go eat breakfast!"

There was more to that guys' getaway than hanging out in the vicinity of topless young women. We took lots of walks along the beach, and I even got the boys into some of the clubs. I don't know what they remember about that trip, but to me, it was a real bonding time for us.

But before they both finally made the commitment to live in Corpus Christi and join me at Magnum, we went through periods when we just didn't have those kinds of opportunities. That's why having them around me every day in our company's office was so important to me. After all those years while I was away traveling for work when they were young, and then everything with the separation and divorce, it was a huge change to suddenly be sharing eight-, nine-, or ten-hour days together, or just driving out to some oilfield site three hours away while shooting the breeze in my pickup.

Around the office, Garrett and Derrick had the self-awareness to realize that calling me "Dad" would not be fitting around the rest of our staff. I certainly didn't want anybody leveraging, saying something like, "Dad said this" or "Dad wants that." The boys asked me for permission to call me Lynn, and that's the way that we handled it.

But we were always aware of our bond, and when we said goodbye at the end of a day or when one of us was leaving on a trip, I began making it a point to tell them, "I love you." In my family growing up, I never heard my dad say that to me until the day he sat me down before I went off to college. Of course I knew he loved me, but we did not feel it was important to say it out loud. We had a mutual understanding of our love for one another. Since that day before college, we did begin to say "I love you" to each other. For me, I just never wanted my sons to wonder. In case something happened, you know.

My father and I were fortunate to have shared quite a few special moments throughout our lives. One that will forever stick with me was in the summer of 2013. As they often did, my parents were visiting my house on North Beach from Port Lavaca. With my mom in the house, Dad and

I were piddling around outside where we felt most comfortable, talking about nothing much at all. It was a beautiful late afternoon. We found ourselves taking a seat on the dock overlooking the canal as the sun began to set to our right. With my Dad next to me, we fell silent, astonished by the beauty of the sunset. He turned to me and said, "I'll be right back." He returned with two ice cold beers and sat down next to me. We cracked the beers open and clanked them together with a "cheers" to the moment. He began to talk about how beautiful everything was, physically and metaphorically; the sunset, the surroundings, and what I had accomplished. He was proud of me and I gushed with happiness.

My father passed away later that fall.

Music has a tendency to earmark memorable events in my life. It was no different after my father's untimely death on September 10th, 2013. On November 11th, after a painful and sorrowful month, Luke Bryan released a song, "Drink a Beer." This song brought me joy in a dark period. It will forever take me back to that moment, when my father and I shared that sunset over a beer, and he told me how proud of me he was.

When the three of us were going over ideas of what to write in this book, Derrick mentioned something about me. He believed that a major part of my motivation in having him and Garrett join me at Magnum was to make up for all that lost time from when they were younger. "Even if Dad does not verbalize this motivation," Derrick said, "all his actions were screaming it."

All I can say is that's probably true. Very, very true. And if music earmarked this memorable moment, it would be the classic song "Cat's in the Cradle," by Harry Chapin.

CHAPTER 7

KEEP IT SIMPLE

When visitors would arrive at Magnum's sprawling complex on Bear Lane in Corpus Christi for the first time, they were likely to notice some of the inspirational sayings posted on the walls of our lobby and inside my office.

"Nothing happens unless first a dream."

The poet Carl Sandburg's words in his poem "Washington Monument by Night" captured the inspiration I felt when I dared to imagine myself running my own company in the oil and gas industry and launched Magnum to try to make it happen. As my career progressed, I made room for new dreams to keep me striving and aspiring.

"The best way to predict the future is to create it."

Peter Drucker, well known for his writings about business management in the mid-1900s, made that phrase popular, although some people believe it can be traced all the way back to Abraham Lincoln. That saying was important to me as an inventor of new tools and products designed to keep us ahead of the curve in the industry. At Magnum, the goal was to create exactly what companies in the oil and gas industry needed so they would need to keep coming back to us for more.

"If it is important to you, you will find a way.
If not, you will find an excuse."

I've always liked that saying from entrepreneur Ryan Blair. It just seems to fit the beliefs that I carried with me from growing up on the farm to making my college football team as a walk-on to all my growth as a business professional. There were never any excuses around my dad, or Coach Steinke, and that's still how I think about anything that I set out to do today.

"The Bumblebee Cannot Fly: according to recognized aero technical tests, the bumblebee cannot fly because of the shape and weight of his body in relation to the total wing area. But the bumblebee doesn't know this, so he goes ahead and flies anyway."

Mary Kay Ash, founder of Mary Kay Cosmetics, reworks Igor Sikorsky's original words in this shorter version of the quote saying: "Aerodynamically, the bumblebee shouldn't be able to fly, but the bumblebee doesn't know it so it goes on flying anyway." The argument may have earlier roots, but whatever way it comes out, it makes me smile and nod. I always understood that for our company to thrive in the marketplace, we had to feel confident that we could create and sell products that others might not believe possible.

In an earlier chapter, I shared the connection I felt to the verse about "The Uncommon Man," which back in the 1950s was referred to as "An American's Creed." When I think about some of the other impactful phrases that helped Magnum to soar higher and higher, I should start with, well, the most basic one:

"Keep It Simple, Stupid."

I first came upon the KISS principle in some business book. It began to make its way around the business community not long after aircraft engineer Kelly Johnson coined the term in the 1960s. His idea was that simplicity should be a primary goal in the design process. Right away, I understood how perfectly this principle described our approach to what we were doing at Magnum.

When we first made our mark in the oil and gas industry with our tubing conveyed perforating tools used in the explosives process of well completion operations, we knew that we had to keep everything very, very simple. One mistake, any "little" accident, could have devastating consequences. My belief was that if we kept our product's design and the way it was utilized as simple as possible, the people using it would not have to think so hard while running high-risk jobs on location during completion operations. I was always sweating out what could go wrong on any operation we were involved in, but if I had confidence that we had kept things as simple as possible, I would sweat a little less.

Devising tools that aimed to keep things simple also helped to give us a competitive advantage. The better I got to know the industry, the more I could see that many of the big guys in oil and gas tended to create and market very complicated tools, which often led to very complicated issues. Well, I couldn't afford those kinds of issues. More important, I discovered that when I really listened to customers describe the perfect tool that would be both simple to use and highly effective, I would come away with something that made sense in a very basic way, did the job, and made them feel like the hero I wanted them to be when they brought that tool or product out into the oilfield.

Since the KISS principle perfectly named my own goals as designer of our tools, I was determined to make sure that it guided everyone else involved in what we were doing at Magnum. If you walked into almost any of our meetings at any stage of creation, development, marketing, or sales of one of our products, there was a pretty good chance that at some moment you would find me shaking my finger as I smiled and said, "Let's remember the KISS principle here." In other words, don't weigh the design and the message down with unnecessary complications.

My reminder would usually be met with a chorus of, "We remember!" I really knew that my team took this principle to heart when I would present some new tool or piece of equipment that I had been designing and somebody would say, "Now, Lynn, remember the KISS principle."

Additionally, I would encourage my team to remember and envision the dirty, crude, and unforgiving conditions our tools would be used in. I would always tell our people that "those wireline hands could tear up a ball bearing with a rubber mallet," and this again drove home our KISS mantra.

Keepin' things simple was a guiding force that went beyond our approach to designing and developing tools. You could say that the basic KISS idea really fit my overall approach to leading and managing a company that grew to a nearly 200-person workforce.

I just never believed in high-sounding, complex management philosophies. The way I looked at it, I had learned almost everything I needed about effective and successful leadership from the day-to-day example of my Mom, Dad, Coach Steinke, and my college football teammates at Texas A&I–Kingsville.

When folks would stop in to see me in my office, they couldn't miss the Hall of Fame plaque commemorating the two back-to-back national championship teams I played for with the Javelinas. If they asked me about it, I was quick to point out that it wasn't just the pride of playing for a championship team that led me to hang that plaque. It was also my way of honoring the foundation I received that has guided me in my business leadership.

Keepin' It Simple

"There's no 'I' in team," I would consistently remind everyone who was a part of Magnum. "And we're all on the same team here. Everybody's contribution counts."

This understanding was critical in gaining and maintaining a high level of success in what we were doing. It didn't matter what anyone's particular job might be. If you were putting a tool together, you had to put it together the proper way. If you didn't, you would be letting the whole team down. If you were running a tool in the field, you had to run it the right way or you would not only undermine the success of that particular operation; you'd be pulling the rest of the company down too.

I wanted to create an environment like our national championship football teams, where everybody felt that we had one another's backs. One way that I tried to mold that kind of environment was to communicate my belief that nobody on our team was better than anybody else. And no matter what anyone's individual role, title, or responsibility may have been, nobody was more important than anybody else.

As the leader of Magnum, I knew it was up to me first and foremost to demonstrate that this was true. It helped that my personality just naturally lends itself to feeling comfortable and at ease around all my employees, with all their different functions and particular personalities. I always wanted everybody who worked for us to feel valued, cared for, and important.

If you followed me around the Magnum complex on a typical day, you might find me at one moment grabbing a broom and helping guys sweep up the warehouse. The next moment you might see me approach a group of employees putting tools into boxes and immediately offer to lend a hand, making it a point to tell them, "If I'm screwing up here, just tell me."

Whenever I took the time to tour our facility, which I tried to do regularly, I would make sure to shake a lot of hands. I would stick around long enough to ask folks how they were doing and thank them for their contributions. I'd listen to them if they wanted to share some personal news with me, like the birth of their first child, the new house they just bought, or the vacation they had enjoyed in Mexico.

I have so many great memories of conversations like that. One day I stopped to chat with one of my employees who immediately pulled me outside to the Magnum parking lot.

"Look at that car," he said with a proud smile.

"Shoot, that's a brand-new Camaro!" I gushed.

"That's the first new car I've been able to buy in my whole life," he said with a big smile. "You wouldn't believe how happy my wife is with me."

After hearing stories like that about how working at Magnum had changed the life of somebody on our team, I would be wiping off a tear as I walked back to my office. I had the same kind of feeling the day I was out somewhere in Corpus Christi and a woman from my staff spotted me and called me over to meet her daughter. After my employee introduced me as her boss, I bent down real close to that little girl and said, "You should be very proud of what your mama is doing. She's really helping us be successful." That little girl looked at me with the biggest smile, then turned and looked at her mother with even bigger smile of pride.

I loved showing my appreciation to our team through our staff parties and gatherings. If we were celebrating somewhere off-site, we would mount our barbecue pit, which was shaped like a .44 Magnum, on a trailer. I can't tell you all the looks we'd get parading that thing down the street when it was all lit up at night.

Our Christmas parties were always the favorite event of the year. We started out at the Republic of Texas on the twentieth floor of the Omni Hotel, overlooking Corpus Christi Bay. We outgrew that venue and moved to the private yacht, The Princess II, in the Corpus Christi marina, the Ortiz Center, and ultimately moved on to the American Bank Center on the Corpus Christi waterfront. We'd always have some kind of fun or motivational theme. I remember the Vegas party when we handed out tickets designed as money to gamble with. When we put on our 1980s theme party, my hoarding finally paid off and I got to dust off my red Hawaiian shirt and jeans to dress up like Tom Selleck in *Magnum, P.I.*

Sometimes I'd get a bunch of guys from work together and rent a bus on a Sunday to head up to Dallas or Houston for a Cowboys or Texans game. For our female team members, Trish would fly with them to the Florida Keys, Las Vegas, or San Francisco. I'd have to say the women got the better of the deal there!

One of the most memorable gifts I have ever received and was proud to display in my office at Magnum was a simple lampshade given to me by my team. That lampshade was covered with copies of dozens of my patents for the tools I created for our company. It was their way of acknowledging me, to thank me for igniting the engine that roared down the tracks of success that benefitted all of us.

For a family-type of operation like ours, it was always important to hire the right kind of people. Even as Magnum got bigger, I had a feel for making good choices. I rarely had to fire anybody, although there were occasions when I might decide that we needed to move someone to a new position. Even then, I tried to make that person feel valued. "My bad," I would say. "We just put you in the wrong place. Let's try this."

As our profits grew, I maintained my commitment to reward my employees with generous bonuses. I also added a full fitness center to our office complex. I understood that all our employees needed to feel valued and appreciated for what they contributed to this Magnum team. And I tried to lead with a velvet glove rather than an iron fist.

My sons Garrett and Derrick certainly had a close-up view of how I managed my leadership role every day during our years together at Magnum. To help flesh out the picture of my management style, I asked them to share their perspective:

Derrick's view: "Lynn has that ability and confidence to step into a room with anyone from line workers to CEOs, and to be equally comfortable with any of those groups. The way he can move from speaking to somebody in Receiving one moment and then slide over to the boardroom to lead effective presentations to top-line managers or executives the next moment, he's like a chameleon. He just adapts to whatever the situation is, and whoever the audience is.

"I think Lynn especially appreciates the opportunities he has to get out and talk with the really genuine and appreciative people he finds all over our company. Those folks all see that Lynn drives around in his pickup, not some fancy CEO-type car. After Lynn would spend times just chatting with his employees, it was like he would carry a piece of them back to his office with him, driving him to work harder in pursuing his goals and the goals of our company."

Garrett's view: "People consistently say that Lynn is the most generous, charismatic, and all-around positive guy they've ever worked with or met. Sometimes I would meet with a potential customer or somebody we were starting to work with, and then I'd bring that person back to Lynn's office to meet him. When I'd walk the individual back to their car afterward, he or she would tell me, 'I had no idea how easy your dad is to get along with. And he tells the best stories!' Whenever Lynn would sit down with somebody new, his personality would always shine through."

This way of being comfortable around different kinds of people, in all kinds of situations, is not something I had to read about in some leadership expert's book and then try to copy. It's just me. I've always enjoyed finding ways to remind everyone that I was no more important than any of them. At the same time, I knew that I had to demonstrate that I was always reliable, that I would keep my word about something I had committed to do.

Another important factor that helped me successfully lead our company was my devotion to the oil and gas industry. Now, I understand that people have different viewpoints about our industry, but my beliefs and opinions have always been clear and consistent. We provide a vital service to the country, and we do it with a commitment to everyone's well-being.

I have to shake my head when I hear some of the myths about the oil industry. With fracking, you hear all these stories about catastrophic environmental damage we're supposedly causing. They talk about contaminating water tables and all kinds of other stuff. Well, I've worked in this industry for thirty-five years, and I know that these harmful things that others complain about just do not happen. There are strict regulations that we always need to follow, and our operations are routinely inspected by the government to ensure that we're consistently adhering to the allowed procedures.

I know that many people outside the industry talk about how we all need to go green, but I can say from everything that I have seen and experienced close-up, that just can't happen. We will always have the need for oil and gas. Without it, how are you going to get from one place to the next? How do you send merchandise from point A to point B? How do you fly from one country to the next? How do you bring cargo ships into a harbor to deliver vital goods? Without oil and gas, our world would get very small.

Within our industry, I've always tried to show the same respect and consideration for any of our vendors and customers, no matter how small or how big. When it would fit to do so, I would try to support others who were also seeking to grow. Back in the 1990s, I consulted for an oil and gas company called Prime Perforating Services in Canada and offered some patents specifically to assist them in their work. Norm and Angela Lussier, the owners of Prime, had been incredibly gracious and supportive of me since the day I began working with them. Their personal and professional ethics were inspirational to me and something I will always cherish and be thankful for. Eventually, I opened a branch office for them down in Corpus Christi, where Garrett and I helped establish a new system of loading perforating guns. Even after letting go of our involvement with this company, I was proud to watch their continued success.

As an entrepreneur, I would take a peek outside of our industry every now and then to allow myself to dream or imagine something else I might try. In the early '90s, I flew into Brisbane, Australia, to talk to some important contacts in oil and gas. I don't remember exactly how this got started, but at some point while I was visiting the country, I came up with an idea to sell bottled water drawn from the Australian billabongs. A billabong is the term used to describe the little isolated ponds left behind when a river or creek changes course. In the Australian climate, these billabongs would fill with water for part of the year and then dry up for a while.

My plan was to bottle this water and sell it in the United States. At that time, only Evian and Perrier had begun to dabble in selling bottled water. As I understood the requirements, I would only need to derive 10 percent of my water from these sources to call it billabong water. I got as far as making up the labels and lids for the bottles and zeroing in on the locations for our supply of water. It blew me away that it was going to cost more for the bottle, label, and lid than it would cost for the water! That discovery and a few other complications convinced me to "bottle up" this plan and file it away. Oh, had I only known that within a couple of years

Keepin' It Simple

bottled water would absolutely take off! I guess that I was just meant to remain an oil and gas guy.

So, in that final phase of Magnum's growth, I stayed focused on my leadership role of an expanding and highly profitable company. A company that just happened to include my two sons along with a few other vital and committed players.

I knew that many family businesses come apart when relationships within the family start to get sticky. It's just hard to maintain the bonds of family ties while keeping up the connections needed to sustain a thriving business.

Earlier I mentioned that the three of us decided that it was important for Garrett and Derrick to call me "Lynn" rather than "Dad" around the workplace. If we were going to build a culture in which everyone was seen as being just as important as everybody else, it wouldn't fit for them to call me by a different name that no one else could use.

Another way that I sought to maintain a sense of equality was to give my sons the same kind of freedom that I would grant anyone with similar job functions and responsibilities. As much as possible, I always wanted to empower my people with the opportunity to use their own wisdom and experience to know what was needed and act on it. Both Garrett and Derrick understood that if they saw something that they thought would work well, I'd give them room to run with it.

Of course, there were still those moments when I might have to remind them that "Lynn" was still in charge. I can recall a time or two when I would have to sit them down and say, "Look, guys, you need to understand that we're no longer in a democratic state right now. It's a dictatorship, and I'm the dictator!"

During one period where money in the company got tight, and I was having to make tough calls in looking out for the bottom line, Derrick had an idea for making a change related to his area of responsibility. When I explained that this was not a change that could happen at that time, Derrick pushed back. Even when we tried to talk it through, he just seemed to keep pushing. That's when I made a very tough call for any business owner, especially when the employee in question happens to be your son.

"Okay, here's what's going to happen," I said to Derrick. "You're going to take thirty days off to think about this. I need you to really decide whether you want to come back here and work at Magnum . . . or not."

I knew that it would break my heart if Derrick chose to leave our company, but if that was what he decided he really needed to do, I would have to give him the room to break away. Here's how Derrick described what happened next:

"I called what was happening 'scho-pro,' like being on scholastic probation in school. There was so much going on in my life at the time. My second child was born around then, and I was thinking a lot about my future. It so happened that I got my hair bleached the day after Lynn put me on probation, so it probably looked like I was totally rebelling. That wasn't exactly true. I just knew that I had to sort out what was really important to me.

"I saw a counselor to help me figure it all out. I wondered if this was the time for me to get out from under the shadow of my father and my older brother, but then I asked myself a question: Where was the most personal growth going to happen? Would it come from moving to Ventura, California, and working for a totally different company, being completely independent? Or would it come from climbing right back into the thick of things with my father and brother and finding out how I could work with them while still being myself?

"As part of making my decision, I wrote a letter to my dad. Basically, I told him that I was more interested and concerned with having a relationship as father and son than as boss-employee, and that if our boss-employee relationship was getting in the way of us being close as father and son, I would walk away."

When Derrick gave me that letter, the door was opened for us to talk, for each of us to share what really mattered. Out of that talking, we came to the decision that we absolutely could work effectively together at Magnum and still be close as father and son. I know that we are both glad that this is how it all worked out. And that letter Derrick wrote to me? I still keep it by my bedside.

CHAPTER 8

MISSION ACCOMPLISHED

My plan all along had been to build an innovative, world-renowned oil and gas product and service company, include my boys to show them the ropes and eventually sell Magnum, cash out, and sail off into the sunset. I wanted that satisfaction of building on my dream and then enjoying the rewards of all our efforts. That was the ultimate mission I sought to achieve.

The first time I had an offer that I stopped long enough to consider was back around 2004, before I had both my boys fully on board. I believe the offer was $1.5 million, which at the time sounded like the most money in the world to me. I came close enough to accepting it that I gathered the whole family to our house for supper to prepare for the big change. That night, I gave Garrett and Derrick a framed picture of the words to the Jimmy Buffet song "Barometer Soup." I resonated with his image of plowing the seas and then rolling along in life with the success gained from hard work.

That sale never happened. It never happened because the company pulled out at the last minute. I was devastated, but it was a fortuitous turn of events. Looking back, I can say now that we had a lot more seas to be plowed.

Magnum was still pointing toward new horizons, and there would come a day when we would have the opportunity to earn a good bit more money and greater success when we finally turned over the rudder of our ship.

I'm awfully glad this happened. Before we finally made the decision to sell Magnum Oil Tools International to Nine Energy Service in 2018, the value of our "little" company had grown by countless leaps and bounds. We had steered our way to a level of successes that I could never have dreamed possible. And all along the way, in addition to the hard work everyone in our company poured in day after day, year after year, we also managed to have ourselves a whole lot of fun.

I may not remember all the details of those final years together, but I sure can recall how good it felt to see what was happening. It's always a treat to take a moment to reflect back on some of the highlights.

I continued to gain satisfaction from coming up with new tools and products to serve the oilfield operations of our customers. I was not obtaining as many new patents, mostly because the legal process had become much more complicated. I remember the time that we went to court against a company that copied one of our tools but wound up losing because of what seemed like a small technicality. As it was explained to me, we had made our case using the phrase "a plug" in referring to our product when we should have used the phrase "the plug" to legally differentiate what was ours.

Still, even if I wasn't always able to put the official stamp of a patent on what I designed, I kept on the lookout for opportunities to create something new. One opportunity emerged after we had been successfully selling our composite frac plugs for quite some time. I was sitting at a meeting with some of my Magnum team members when I said, "Wouldn't it be neat if we could come up with some new plug, something where you hit some kind of button or some kind of activation, and then, bang, the plug would just disappear?" My previous experience with explosives used in oilfield operations was feeding this idea.

Now that we had the goal, we had to figure out the steps needed to fulfill it. Could we find the right material that would make this new plug disappear in the way that I imagined? Our composite frac plug was made of fiberglass, but this new plug was going to need something very different.

I sent my team out looking for answers, and I was excited to hear the results. While Garrett and Derrick were attending an oil and gas trade show, they met some chemical experts from Japan who offered a possible solution: polyglycolic acid, or PGA for short. This was the same material used in stitches to repair a cut or a wound in our bodies.

When I sat down with some folks from the Kureha Corporation, I said, "Okay, so this PGA dissolves in five or six days in the body, with its 98.6 temperature. But can it dissolve in about the same time at the 250-degree temperature of an oil well?"

"Yes, we can make it do that," they responded.

Through a strategic partnership with Magnum, Kureha helped support our efforts in scaling the product to commercialization to meet the market demand. Our first objective was to prove out the performance of the material in a downhole application. I reached out to a friend who worked for a company that was the leader in the market of sliding sleeve well completion technology. After some outrageous success with the frac ball in proof of concept and in the market, our next step was to make a dissolvable frac plug.

Knowing the material's capabilities and limitations, we were ready for this phase. The boys and I worked with my team of engineers to create the design. Once we had the initial concept manufactured, we thoroughly tested the prototype at our outside test lab designed to simulate downhole wellbore conditions. Sure enough, it worked just as we had pictured in our minds the first time, and it was ready to be run by some of the early adopters of this technology. The idea was that with this product we would be able to eliminate risk and cost during coil tubing methods of milling out composite plugs. With a dissolvable frac plug, customers could set the plug, isolating zones during plug and perf, and the plug would begin to dissolve shortly after they got their frac off. Once their frac was completed, they could get to production much sooner while minimizing risk and reducing cost. This would happen because our product would dissolve into the wellbore with little to no debris left behind.

Our dissolvable frac plug had just been born! I was confident this groundbreaking tool was positioned to become our next big thing, but we didn't know just how big it would be.

We knew that we needed a highly marketable name for this dissolvable plug, and I plunged right in with my team to choose one. It was always fun to come up with names with the marketing team. Previously we had developed a dissolvable frac ball that we called the Magnum Fastball because it dissolved very fast. We had a robot that manufactured that product, which I decided we should call "Nolan" after Hall of Fame pitcher Nolan Ryan, whose legendary fastball was once clocked at 108 mph. Since Nolan spent most of his career with the Houston Astros, we put an Astros cap on our robot. Remembering how well the Fastball name had clicked, we figured we'd stick with the sports theme for our new dissolvable frac plug. So, we officially launched the Magnum Vanishing Plug, or MVP. Garrett led the marketing campaign that emphasized this plug's value by reducing costs, risks, and time at the well site. Once again, we had a signature product propelling our company to new heights.

Before calling upon sports terms to name our products, we had a long history of tapping many familiar names linked to Magnum guns. We had the Magnum Snub Nose and the Magnum Long Range, as well as the 357 Magnum and the 44 Magnum. This nomenclature lined up perfectly because the OD, or outer diameter, of our composite plugs needed to match up with the inner diameter, or ID, of the respect casing that our plugs would be set in to achieve the ideal standoff or tolerance to withstand fracking pressure. So the OD of our plugs not only took on the names of these iconic pistols, but they also literally took on the OD of the plugs: The 357 had an

OD of 3.57 and the 44 had an OD of 4.40 to fit and perform into varying casing weights of 4 1/2" and 5 1/2" (pounds/feet) respectively. I always believed that coming up with names should enhance your marketability while also bringing a smile of recognition to everybody who heard them. I never did forget how dressing up like the star of *Magnum, P.I.* opened doors for me in those early days when doors were pretty darn hard to open. I always liked to call this the "sticky" factor.

We also kept our eyes out for opportunities to have a good time while effectively courting potential customers or building relationships with established clients. A while ago, Garrett reminded me of how we had gained access to one of those private boxes at Cowboys Stadium (later renamed AT&T Stadium) for Dallas Cowboys games. We couldn't afford to actually buy one of those private boxes, which I believe went for close to a million bucks at the time, but we had contacts who agreed to lease us their box when they weren't using it. We hosted some memorable parties while getting to meet some Hall of Fame Cowboys players. And, of course, we were strategic about who we invited into "our" private box.

One Sunday the Cowboys were hosting the Denver Broncos. It so happened that we were seeking the business of clients from Denver at the time, so we flew them in and spared no expense in wining and dining them at the game. The Broncos prevailed in an epic shootout between two future Hall of Fame quarterbacks: Tony Romo and Peyton Manning. The final score was 51–48, and although the Magnum crew were all Cowboys fans, I can't say that we were all that disappointed, since the victory helped to pump up the spirits of our guests from Denver. Feeling good about the whole day, they awarded us a multimillion-dollar contract.

On another occasion, we invited some targeted prospects from West Virginia to Corpus Christi. From what we had heard, these guys had hardly ever ventured out of the state of West Virginia before and had spent little if any time on the ocean. No problem. After driving them out to Padre Island for a big, fancy dinner, we took them on an offshore fishing expedition. Garrett is our family expert on the ways of Gulf water fishing, and he made sure these folks caught more than their share of billfish, kingfish, snapper, and mahi. We took lots of photos with these West Virginians proudly holding up their prized catch, and I'm sure they loved sharing them with the folks back home. Of course, the big "catch" of the day was the major contract we reeled in for Magnum!

Sometimes I would invite potential or committed customers out on my own private yacht. When I'd show them around the waterfront areas of Corpus Christi, I always made sure to point out the USS *Lexington Museum* on the bay, our city's highly popular exhibit that showcases the famous World War II aircraft carrier.

I didn't think twice about continuing this habit the day that we happened to have ten folks from Japan on board from Kureha, the supplier of our dissolvable material. When I began explaining the history of the *Lexington*, one of my guests frowned. "This boat," he said, "it killed many Japanese people."

Oops! I sat there crawling in my skin, realizing that I should have remembered the natural feelings of those whose ancestors were on the other side of World War II. I began to apologize, but my guest's frown evaporated faster than our Magnum Vanishing Plug. "That was a very long time ago," he said, and we were soon on our way, even sharing a laugh about something else that we spotted on the tour.

That seemed to be the way it was going more and more often for Magnum during those years of rapid growth and rising profit margins. Our company was thriving, and throwing parties at Cowboys' games or taking customers on ocean fishing expeditions was a lot more fun than all those long days and nights I used to spend sweating out what might happen when our explosives equipment was being put to the test at some far-off oilfield.

However, not all relationships ended well. Sometimes, after some initial success, things would get a bit cross. As a company that was constantly devising and marketing our own new designs and technology, we had to watch out for customers who would start to manufacture copycat products and market them to our other customers behind our back. When we discovered what was happening, we took swift and firm action to stop it. Fortunately, we maintained a network of trusted friends and customers who would act on our behalf by keeping an eye open for this kind of greedy activity engaged in by those trying to capitalize on the magnitude of our success.

While climbing the ranks of the oil and gas industry, we thrived with our underdog mentality. We all had something that gave us extra motivation. I still remembered being laughed at by my own friends and neighbors in 1986 when I shared my plan to build a major business after my humble start. Garrett could still hear the voice of his college marketing professor who told him that he didn't have what it takes to successfully market a company. Derrick had doubters questioning whether he could make room for his passionate beliefs about the ways of the world from a seat inside the oil and gas industry.

Yes, sir, we were carrying a chip on our shoulders, and that chip just helped drive us higher and higher, up toward the inner circle of the industry. We scratched and clawed our way onto championship row.

During those final years, we found ourselves going toe to toe with some of the world's largest and best-known companies: Baker Hughes, Weatherford, Halliburton, Schlumberger. As our footing became stronger, we never felt like we were entering into any negotiation as an inferior party.

We had to summon an extra boost of courage and confidence when we began selling directly to operators in oil and gas more regularly, without relying on the service provider in the middle to buy the products and tools from us and then sell them to the companies out on the well sites. Garrett recently recalled a story about how a big-name company approached us to seek an exclusive distributorship of our composite plugs. We told them very clearly that we would not be tied down that way. Anyone and everyone were our customers.

Going direct to customers operating in the oilfields rather than dealing with the service providers in the middle meant having to expand and reorganize our staff, but we made that adjustment. We made all kinds of adjustments as Magnum grew. If you want to be a successful player in oil and gas, you learn to be flexible—a trait the big boys don't have.

The more we grew and expanded, the more offers to sell we attracted. After that initial offer of about $1.5 million, I believe the next potential deal was for somewhere around $12 million. Again, that money sounded huge to us at Magnum. It was definitely tempting. But then I considered our own rising numbers. We grossed $3 million one year, then $6 million the next year. From that point on, we began to double our annual revenue year after year. That's rapid growth!

Well, we turned down that $12 million offer, and in the following year we *made* $12 million in gross revenue. That told me that we were doing right by hanging on. Three years later, that same company came back with a new offer: $25 million. I thought about that one for a week or two before coming to the only conclusion that seemed to make sense.

"We're still growing like crazy here," I said to myself. "We can't sell."

No more than a few years later, somebody in the industry came knocking on our door again. Would we sell Magnum to them for *$264 million*? When I turned that one down too, some people around me were starting to scratch their heads about just what I was up to here. Yes, sir, I was holding out for, well, something more than I would ever have thought possible when I took my first tool to market and launched my little business back in 1985. Finally, we made the decision to put Magnum on the market.

We called upon a trusted and well-known broker in the industry to represent our company, and we were amazed to hear that about forty credible parties were interested in purchasing Magnum. Some were among the biggest names in the industry. After weeding out many possible suitors, we narrowed the list to about twelve companies that we would bring together to hear our in-person presentation in Houston.

On the way to this pivotal moment, we got caught in some heavy traffic coming up from Corpus Christi, which made us about an hour late to the presentation. Somehow, that just helped to break the ice. Who knows? Maybe it even added to the intrigue of who we were and what we had to offer.

In our individual meetings with each potential buyer, we fielded a barrage of questions and poured through all the data they requested. Some of those meetings went on for several hours.

After long and careful consideration, we pared the list down to three finalists. Eventually, we made the decision to go with Nine Energy Service. After details of the agreement were finalized in October 2018, we had accepted a total compensation package of $493 million. Not exactly what my doubters at my neighborhood party in Oklahoma City back in 1986 were predicting for my future!

Back in the introduction of this book, I described the celebration trip our Frazier family enjoyed on that private yacht in the Bahamas while we were approaching the finish line of the long sales process. That fun excursion was especially gratifying to me because it really marked the fulfillment of not one dream but two. The first dream had been just to start my own company and grow it into something big, profitable, and fulfilling. The second dream was to see that process through to the end point as a shared identity with my sons, Garrett and Derrick. Magnum never could have reached that pinnacle without them.

The boys and I, and our families, still talk about those days on the *Mambo*.

"That trip put everything into perspective," Garrett observes. "It allowed us to celebrate this huge decision while in community with our loved ones. In a way, it felt like the three of us were accountable for this final green light to sell Magnum, and accountable to each other. We had arrived together at our greatest professional achievement."

"It was so exciting to begin to envision what the future might hold for us," notes Derrick. "Smoking some of the smoothest cigars I have ever tasted and drinking some of the best-tasting rum I've ever had, all while enjoying an incredibly beautiful environment, life during those five days just felt smooth as butter."

I mentioned earlier how the three of us enjoyed special moments at sunset at the back of the *Mambo* and that we raised our glasses to toast our success. I did something else to mark this passage point on our father-son journey. I gave both Garrett and Derrick this little poem that I wrote:

My Sons

I sometimes wish you were still small,
Not yet so big and strong and tall.
For when I think of yesterday,
I close my eyes and see you play.
I often miss those little boys,
Who pestered me to buy them toys,
Who filled my days with pure delight,
From early morning 'til late at night.
We watch our children change and grow
As seasons come, and seasons go.
But I remember our life has a perfect plan
To shape these boys into a man.
Today, my sons, I'm proud of you
For all the life and hard work you do.
I'll love you guys 'til my days are done,
And I'm so grateful you're my sons.

—Dad

You know that you've got special kids when they inspire a pretty private guy like me to write his own poem!

Once the sales agreement with Nine Energy was finalized, I had some other important people to welcome into my celebration circle. I gathered my Magnum employees to announce the news.

"Today is a very special and pivotal day in our organization's history," I began. "If you guys will remember, it was just two years ago that we were all together downstairs and I gave you a very emotional talk about our future. We were in a downturn at that time, and I told you that I had been through a few of these downturns in the oil and gas industry and tried my best to assure you that we were going to make it out of that one too. And we did it, with flying colors! And that was thanks to all of you, and all your hard work and dedication that got us where we are today."

On this very special day in the history of Magnum, I shared with my team that story about how I was laughed at by my friends and neighbors when I told them that the company I had only recently launched, and which was going through some typical early struggles, would one day make a real name for itself. They just didn't take me seriously when I proclaimed that Magnum would rise to major heights in the oil and gas industry.

"So, for the past thirty-three years, I have strived to have Magnum set the standard for quality, for design, and for performance in downhole completion tools," I went on to say to our Magnum team. "From our talented people to our product designs, and the structure of our company—everything we have done for the past three decades has been about realizing my dream and building products with purpose. As a result, we have in fact made our mark in oilfields all around the world. Our success has also guaranteed the attention of competitors and some of the largest oilfield service companies in the world."

After taking the time to explain the sale of Magnum to Nine Energy and how the transition would proceed, I tried to express my deep gratitude.

"I want to thank everyone here for your personal contribution in helping us achieve Magnum's success and for helping my dream come true," I said. "And because of all your hard work, I want to reward each and every one of you."

I had been consistently awarding quarterly bonuses, and for this important passage point, I decided to go a step further. Every employee was to receive a transaction bonus. Depending on length of service with our company, this bonus would range from one half of their base annual salary to twice that salary. Under our plan, employees would receive half their bonus at the time of the transition and the other half if they had remained with Nine Energy for one year afterward. I had taken care of my personal family. And now I had taken care of my Magnum family. Only then could I finally say to myself, "Mission accomplished."

WORST OF TIMES

Good afternoon everybody. I really don't know what to say. Today is one of the toughest days ever. No fault of any of us, but . . . the oil and gas industry has dealt us shitty hand. I'm sure everyone here has been following the news and knows just how bad our industry really is. We have gone from over 2000 rigs running in the US this week last year to 842 rigs this week. This is over a 55% drop in rig activity. Not only has the rig activity dropped but these oil companies aren't completing and fracking all the wells they are drilling. They are waiting to frack and complete these wells when the price of oil increases. Also last year this month, September, we did over 15 million dollars in revenue for the month. This September, we are going to be lucky to do 3.5 million.

We are in hell right now, we are in hell. I just want to rally everyone and tell everyone to keep your chin up. But we as a team must do everything we can to keep fighting to weather this storm. We have over

Mission Accomplished

150 Magnum families here to take care of. 150. We can hang our heads and sit around and wait to see what life is gonna deal us next or we can step up, work our asses off, pulling together to fight and claw our way back to make the absolute best out of this bad situation. If we all pull together we will claw our way back I assure you. Now it ain't gonna be easy. But it can be done if we all work together. You want to know why I feel so strongly we can claw back? Because we have a helluva team here. We Are Magnum!

I look around and see all you young, energetic, enthusiastic people and it is so inspiring. Believe it or not I have been here in very similar situations several times before when the oil industry decided to take a dump and make life a living hell. Maybe not quite this bad or involving so damn many people but very similar none the less. But I want to assure everyone here that I and many of our Magnum leaders can and will do everything in our power to help lead us out of this hell we are in. And I need everyone of you team members step up and help as well. I don't ever want to go through anything like this again!

You know when you get old you realize you have been taught a lot and you have learned a lot over the years. You have many, many experiences in this crazy place called life, some good, some not so good. You see a lot of situations and there are many times when you just have to say that things happen for a reason. And then you just gotta pick yourself up, dust yourself off, and keep your head up and keep going. This is one of those situations, there's nothing we can do but make the best out of this. Look around at each other. These are your teammates. We're all in this together. Everyone here should see a teammate that is willing to do anything to make us at Team Magnum a success and help us claw out of this hell. A day at a time . . . everybody . . . a day at a time. This is the oil and gas industry, it will cycle back, it's just a matter of when.

continued

And in the meantime, we must keep our head on a swivel to find more opportunity. We must work with expedience and purpose and we must work smarter.

We as Team Magnum need to take this a day at a time and not only will we survive . . . we will come out a winner, each and every one of us will win! I want to thank all of you for your hard work and continued support here at Magnum! Thank you.

CHAPTER 9

THE FRAZIER FAMILY LEGACY

It was a very familiar scene. The sun was going down, and I was seated in a comfortable Corpus Christi restaurant looking out over the waters of Corpus Christi Bay. Across the table sat a gentleman who had a keen interest in one of my creative design ideas. As we waited for our dinner to arrive, we talked for a while, bouncing possibilities back and forth as we searched for the best approach to accomplish what was needed.

Then, to make my thoughts clearer, I unwrapped the silverware inside my napkin, laid that napkin down flat on the table, and began to draw my design concept with the pen I kept tucked in my shirt pocket. After sliding the napkin over to my dinner companion, I watched him hold it up to the light and proclaim, "That's it exactly!"

Yes, I was still drawing my design ideas on napkins. But while that part of this scene was familiar, there were some pretty big differences between what was going on early that evening and what I had been doing for thirty-three years at Magnum.

First, I owned that restaurant that we happened to be sitting in. Fajitaville, located on historic North Beach in Corpus Christi, features signature fajitas, seafood, and burgers, along with beachside bar service and games, an outdoor stage, and a Ferris wheel. Not exactly what you would expect from an oil and gas guy.

Second, that fellow sitting across the table may have been a Texan like me, and he also happened to work on projects all across the state and even around the world. But Jeff Blackard doesn't work in the oil industry. He's a world-renowned real estate developer.

Finally, that design I was sketching on my napkin was not some new tool or product that would make an oil company's operations run more safely and smoothly. No, it actually depicted part of the vision Jeff and I shared to totally revamp and revitalize the North Beach area.

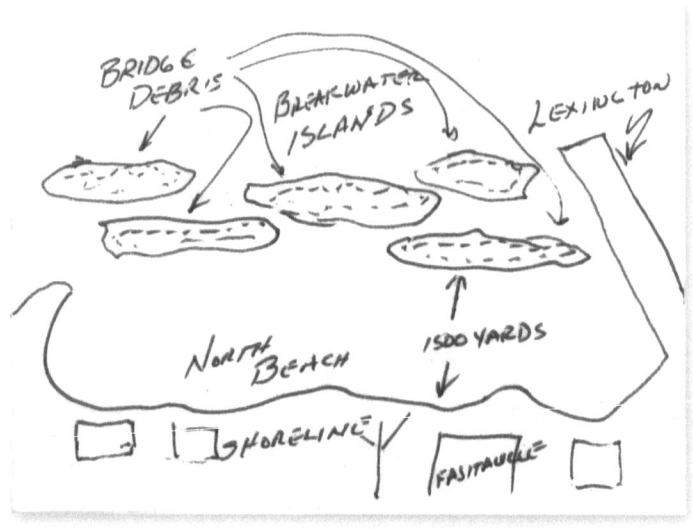

As anyone who's been around Corpus Christi for a while knows, North Beach back in the 1920s, '30s, and '40s, was a real hot spot for locals and tourists from all over Texas and beyond. North Beach was somewhere to see and be seen, with the usual beachy hotels, restaurants, ice cream and souvenir shops, along with tattoo parlors, a boardwalk, a public saltwater pool, a beachside roller coaster, and a Ferris wheel. During the World

War II era, soldiers from the many military bases in the area would flock to North Beach, and so did the young women who hoped to meet one. Romances blossomed, dreams were hatched, and Corpus Christi really had something to be proud of.

Then the causeway came in linking the mainland to North Padre Island, cutting off most of the regular traffic along North Beach. Drainage and flooding became nasty problems, and what used to be a fun and lively place became a blight and still is today.

But whether it's oil and gas or something else, I'm a guy who always believes in possibilities. People like Jeff Blackard, myself, and many others envision a reborn North Beach that will someday earn back the title of "The Beacon of South Texas."

Our plans feature the construction of a grand canal, following a concept modeled after San Antonio's famous River Walk. Corpus Christi has a rich history, but it's often referred to as the city that got left behind while places like San Antonio, Houston, and Dallas-Fort Worth rose in population and status over the last few decades. It's exciting to imagine how a feature like the River Walk in conjunction with a beach can open doors for residences, hotels, restaurants, and other businesses and attractions that could make Corpus Christi really come alive, living up to its nickname as the "Sparkling City by the Sea."

I'm eager to play a significant role in these advances for our city. I've been invested in the future of North Beach for years already. My gold-colored house that I mentioned earlier is located in a neighborhood on North Beach. I own a couple of other residential properties nearby. In addition to Fajitaville, the restaurant that I launched, I also bought and refurbished the Hotel De Ville right next door. And down at one end of the beach, Jeff Blackard and I are partnering to develop Lighthouse Pointe, a 160-unit apartment complex and stone village that will feature boat slips and a 164-foot-tall lighthouse. We imagine that lighthouse as a beacon that will welcome locals and visitors to the new North Beach.

A valued and dear relationship that gave me quite a bit of support with the North Beach endeavors was with Mike and Janet Railsback. Janet is my cousin from my mom's side. Both Mike and Janet were incredibly positive and supportive. They were instrumental in managing the North Beach Investments, Fajitaville, Hotel de'Ville, and Marinaville. They kept an eye on the day-to-day operations and made sure that all North Beach operations ran smoothly. Tragically, Janet's dad's health began to deteriorate. As a result, Mike and Janet decided to move back to help. There aren't many days that go by that I don't miss our afternoon cocktails and conversations with them. They are both incredibly positive and supportive people I love being around.

There's been a real buzz in the media about these creative ideas and proposed projects in the last year or two. If you sit down with anybody old enough to remember the popular seaside haven that North Beach once was, or those who flock to the area from March to November these days to visit the USS *Lexington* or the Texas State Aquarium, they'll light up when you show them the pictures of what North Beach can be and hopefully will soon become.

I feel energized and proud to have my name linked to something that will serve so many people. Although I didn't grow up in Corpus Christi, it's been my home for twenty years. I want to be a part of this city becoming the best that it can be.

For the same reason, I also bought a 40,000-square-foot office building in downtown Corpus Christi after we sold Magnum. Located at 807 North Upper Broadway, this historic structure was once the headquarters of the Texas grocery giant H-E-B before it moved to San Antonio. The building has been vacant for thirty-five years, and although other folks have talked about plans for something new there every now and then, nothing has ever gotten off the ground. Like with the revitalization of North Beach, I'm determined to take this place that people in the city are familiar with from the past and turn it into something attractive and memorable for the present and future.

The Frazier Family Legacy

My plans for this four-story building include a rooftop events venue on top, with a glass wall all around that will open up an expansive view of the bay. Our project also features a coffee shop and retail businesses, along with office space for a wide spectrum of businesses. We may put in a bar or lounge in the basement. The third floor will most likely house the main office of the Frazier Companies, the umbrella entity that now manages my various ventures beyond the oil and gas industry. While the interior will look modern and spacious, we're going to keep the original exterior façade that dates back to 1953 when the building was constructed for the Southern Minerals Corporation.

I remember when downtown Corpus Christi was a vibrant place. During my days as a college student in Kingsville, I would come there mostly for the restaurants and clubs, but I also noted the many corporate office buildings that helped give the area more life. Now I want to help bring that life and vitality back to downtown, as another way to help the city pivot from that period when Corpus Christi just seemed to fall by the wayside.

Refurbishing this office building is one of my many new dreams for projects that I may develop and then look back and say, "This is what can be done." That's the same spirit that propelled me to launch and grow Magnum. But these development projects at North Beach and downtown Corpus Christi will add another dimension to my dreams and visions: They will have the Frazier name linked to them.

Since that time when it became clear that we would finally be selling Magnum, I began to feel a greater desire to leave a legacy. My dad passed away in 2013. Lester Frazier and my mom, Lynda, worked hard and accomplished a great deal in their lives, and his collection and sales of exotic birds was a very creative enterprise. Their hard work and ambition allowed all of us to have a wonderful and full life. And although I accomplished something special with my leadership of Magnum Tools International, it didn't have my name on it. Now I've just reached the point where I want to take this next step.

I'm thinking of my family moving through current and future generations. I have Garrett and Derrick, and they have their kids now, and there will be future generations that also will be part of this Frazier clan. When it gets to be twenty years, forty years, or even sixty years down the road, I just think it would be great if children and young adults in our family could look at this office building, or Lighthouse Pointe, or Fajitaville, or the Hotel De Ville, or anything else that's visible, attractive, important, and has my name on it and say, "Hey, look what Grandpa (or Great-Grandpa or maybe even Great-Great-Grandpa!) did. Maybe I could do something like that someday too."

They could take away the understanding that you can come from little or nothing and still make something of yourself if your attitude is positive and your drive is strong enough. I'm just one example of how true that is in our great country.

Just the thought of playing any role in the growth and personal success of other Fraziers or other extended family members really touches me. That's what steered me into inviting Garrett and Derrick into Magnum, to help show them how they could aspire to something bigger and greater than what they might have imagined.

Family remains very important to me. I realize that with my freedom and financial security, I could choose to live anywhere in the world. And believe me, I know some very beautiful and attractive places. But it feels even more important to me at my age and time in life that I stay close to family. And I'm still a Texas boy at heart.

In terms of my Frazier family heritage, I always felt that I had missed out on something because I had never been able to learn much about my father's ancestors. I did get to visit my grandfather's tombstone in western Colorado once. I brought my boys and my dad with me, too, and we were able to walk away with a priceless photo representing four generations of Fraziers.

I know that somewhere along the family trail, the Fraziers immigrated from Scotland. To gain a greater sense of connection to the long-ago past, some of our family members have done some genealogical research. They're still working on that. I also took some time to trace the Frazier family crest when we set up a foundation to manage some of the proceeds from the sale of Magnum. I already had been told by one of my dad's older brothers that our family name was once spelled Fraser, with the "s" kind of scribbled. Apparently, when the name was written on the ship manifest on behalf of one of my ancestors coming over to America, it was transcribed as "Frazier." That spelling of the name stuck.

Historically, the Scottish clan name of Fraser or Frazier dates back to the twelfth century. I learned that Sir Simon Fraser was known as "the Scottish patriot" and was a commander under Sir William Wallace during the 1302 Battle of Rosin, where the Scots defeated three regiments of the English army. The original family crest depicted strawberries because the clan was at one time known as "strawberry bearers." My sons and I decided to include that image when we remade the family crest. And, yes, I do like strawberries.

I've definitely kept busy since selling Magnum. I've got those new Corpus Christi development projects going, and I maintained offices at Nine Energy Service during an initial transition period. The good news is that I can often leave work after normal business hours now, and I don't take it home with me so much. Heck, I haven't even been keeping up with how to operate the latest versions of AutoCAD.

With a bit more time on my hands, I've had the chance to reconnect with some old friends I had not seen in decades. My girlfriend Anne and I do a bit more socializing, sometimes hosting gatherings at our home. When our guests step inside our social room, they are greeted by a sign welcoming them to "The Fraziers' Bar & Grill." The pool just off the patio door features a waterfall and a firepit, and on my dock, they can spot my forty-six-foot Sundancer with its sticker off the stern that says, "Keep Fracking My Friends."

On the walls inside the house, there's a large, framed photo of Fajitaville taken above from a helicopter and seven clocks displaying the current time in seven different locations around the world. The clock that says "Fajitaville" is always set at five o'clock. You know, happy hour. I keep that one near my "Jimmy Buffet for President" sign.

Since my name has become much more public through the sale of Magnum and my involvement with major Corpus Christi projects, I have to carefully screen all the invitations that come pouring in from many parts of our community. That's the downside to being in the limelight, but there is a definite plus: Having a greater name recognition has opened more doors for me to connect with people who may be in a position to support me with some of my new projects. Or maybe just introduce me to new exciting ideas.

I also make sure to carve out plenty of time to get out on the water in my big ol' boat. I have to admit that I enjoy cranking up my music now and again out there. In fact, there's a story I like to tell about that.

As those of us in Corpus Christi know well, the famous Tejano singer Selena (full name Selena Quintanilla-Perez) spent part of her childhood and many years of her stardom in Corpus Christi before she was tragically killed a few weeks before her twenty-fourth birthday. Whenever I'm taking folks out in my boat, I make it a point to swing by the Mirador de la Flor, also known as Selena's Seawall. This life-sized bronze statue of Selena wearing a leather jacket looking out toward Corpus Christi Bay has been a popular tourist attraction ever since it was sculpted a few years after Selena's death.

When we pull close, I tell my passengers, "There's the Selena statue," as I raise the volume level to "Como La Flor," "Bidi Bidi Bom Bom," or one of Selena's other big hits. With my speakers on the front of my boat blaring the music, people by the statue can't help but turn their heads our way. It's not unusual to see these Selena fans immediately start dancing and singing along. It's great fun! Some people who know me say they expect to hear that I've become a city tour boat captain someday. Heck, who knows? I'm already a member of the Corpus Christi Convention and Visitors Bureau.

Around North Beach, some folks know me as the guy who rakes the beach to keep the sand nice and smooth and cleaned of debris. I've got my own good-sized tractor with a rake on the back and Fajitaville stickers on the side, and I just go out there with my earphones plugged in, listening to music and taking care of what needs to be done. If the beach is left unattended, sometimes the seaweed can get knee-deep. If my rake pulls up any seaweed, I just take it and dump it in some other area where it decomposes. People who know me sometimes look at me kind of funny. "Couldn't you get some other guy to rake the beach for you?" they ask. Heck no, I've been driving tractors since my dad sent me out in the fields when I was nine years old. It's just in my blood.

Anyway, I find those hours of cleaning up the beach to be very relaxing. I just like the beach to look really nice, and I'm not sure I could trust somebody else to do a good enough job. We still have a fair number of visitors from far inland Texas locales who enjoy coming to North Beach to wade in the ocean waters, and it's the site of events that attract hundreds of people from our community. It was during the annual Polar Bear Plunge on New Year's Day, when people plunge into the chilly water of Corpus Christi Bay to benefit the ALS Therapy Institute, that I met my girlfriend Anne. She braved the water, I didn't, but we hit it off.

When I look down the road at operating our Lighthouse Pointe apartments, I imagine myself managing the maintenance. I've got experience in that arena from my college days, and heck, I still look out for ways to save a dollar.

I will spend money on travel, and when I choose to leave Texas these days, it's because I want to, not because I need to for my business. I make regular visits to the Caymans, a place I fell in love with when I was first introduced to it about fifteen years ago. There's something about the beautiful beaches, the calm waters, and the easygoing vibe from the locals and tourists alike. One of the first times I was there, I decided to check with the residents to see if there was anything off about my image of this "perfect" place. In my experience, the best people to ask those questions are the taxi drivers.

"So, tell me," I said to my taxi driver one day, "what is it that you DON'T like about the Caymans?"

"Oh, that's easy," he said. "It's the same temperature all the time."

I had to laugh. In my house, the thermostat is set at a constant seventy-four or seventy-five degrees. If I could set the outside thermostat to the same mild temperature, like the averages in the Caymans of about eighty-eight in the day and seventy-five at night, I'd do that in a heartbeat. Didn't sound like much of a downside to me!

I bought a condo on the Caymans a while ago, and I love taking people down there to share it. At Christmastime, I normally gather together a big family group at my home on North Beach—my parents, sister and two brothers and their spouses, aunts and uncles, nieces and nephews, and other extended family—and after hanging out long enough to exchange gifts in Texas, I fly to the Caymans to keep the party going in the fun and sun until New Year's.

I also bought a place in Costa Rica. Garrett likes to drag me down there sometimes and include me in his offshore fishing expeditions. And once a year, usually around Valentine's Day, we head to the Miami area for a big boat show. When I head off on any of these trips, it sure is nice not to have to worry about checking in on the operations of some oil rig.

I'm not the only one in this Frazier clan who has found himself wading in new waters in the aftermath of our lucrative sale of Magnum. Both Garrett and Derrick have been navigating their own personal and professional changes over the last couple of years. Once again, I'll leave it to them to describe what that's been like.

Life after Magnum for Derrick

For many years while working with my dad and my brother, I held on to this idea that Magnum was the means to an end. I figured I would work there until I was about forty and then take a look around and begin to decide what I really wanted to do next. But Magnum became more than that to me. Then the sale went down and the winds began to shift. Life didn't continue down the path I had envisioned; things got a bit blurry and became clear all at once. It wasn't the way that I imagined it. All of a sudden, the Magnum colors and the Magnum brand that everyone in my family knew so well were beginning to shift and contrast.

The change came at a time when my life already was starting to get pretty crazy. We had our third child, Sullivan, and we were building a new house in our same neighborhood, just on a different street, a touch closer to our friends. With regard to the house, my wife, Ryan, used to be a construction manager, so she was a huge asset to have around the project. She was heavily involved and drove the project that we both loved being a part of with precision and clarity. We work really well together, with my interests for interior design and her commitment to project management.

After the sale of Magnum to Nine Energy Service, I stayed on in my role as product manager.

I was certain that this could be another opportunity for me to shine within Nine Energy. Regarding their completion tool division, their products and processes needed help; they needed that level of sophistication my team and I cultivated at Magnum. Nine Energy had the intentions to invest in the leaders at Magnum and lay out a path for us to be successful within the organization. However, this didn't take hold immediately nor over the course of my time there. I couldn't identify exactly why this wasn't happening, but I had to chalk it up to the fact that things take time to develop. Certainly, there has to be a correlation between magnitude and duration: the greater the impact, the longer it will take. I knew that the impact and success I was chasing and craving wasn't going to happen overnight. The patience required to make real change at a corporate level coupled with another oil downturn and tough cost-cutting decisions eventually led me to decide to embark on my next chapter and separate from Nine Energy. During my nineteen months there, I learned a tremendous amount and loved my time with most of the individuals there. However, I knew that this was my time to "throw off the bowlines... explore. Dream. Discover."

So, life's been crazy, for sure, but it's been fun and exciting, too. When I take a moment to look back, just to say I am thankful for everything that has happened in being part of the team at Magnum and helping to bring it to the place we arrived at wouldn't be sufficient. I may not know the road map ahead in my life for the next five years or longer, but I'm trying to be okay with that. It helps to look at the process as being swept up in waves of excitement and opportunity, as opposed to being tied down by fear and limitation.

I know that my dad would like for Garrett and me to stay connected to what he's started and will continue to do with Frazier Companies. That's definitely something to consider, but I'm also holding that same question I have asked myself before: Do I stay on this path of working with my family or do I pursue something new and different? I'm doing my best to weigh different choices and opportunities. Engaging in new educational pursuits remains one of many roads I might follow.

Sometimes I wish I knew exactly what was going to happen, but then I pull myself back to riding those waves of uncertainty. It helps to remember the words of Mary Poppins in the movie *Mary Poppins Returns*:

*"We're on the brink of an adventure, children.
Don't spoil it with questions."*

Life after Magnum for Garrett

In one way or another, Magnum has been a part of nearly my entire life. In the beginning of my full-time career at Magnum, it provided stability and purpose for me as a young man. Additionally, Dad and I were able to begin the process of making up for the lost times during my adolescence, and I'm so thankful our relationship has grown, strengthened, and developed into what it is today. There were times, however, that the effort required didn't come without sacrifice. I remember back in 2009, while navigating my first downturn in the oil industry, our sales staff was small and I knew I would need to travel a great deal throughout the United States to hustle sales, grow our market share, and get the Magnum name out in a way that the industry had never seen before. My daughter Olivia was born that year, and my wife, Trish, would often say, "You were on the road for all of Olivia's first year." I was doing whatever it took to gain market share and grow Magnum, but I realized that I was sacrificing time with my wife and children in order to do this. I began to understand what might have been going through Dad's thoughts when he was in his thirties. I didn't want my children to experience what it felt like without their father around. However, I knew that it would only be temporary and that it was a means to an end.

When I told my wife and children about our plans to sell Magnum over dinner in the summer of 2018, my son Dylan let out an indignant, "WHAT?" From the time he was old enough to understand where his dad worked, along with PawPaw and "Uncle D," he would say that one day he would go to work at Magnum too. I would take him to the shop with me from time to time and show him the ins and outs of our operation and teach him about our products. He was so excited on those days and showed a genuine interest in how things clicked around the shop. This made me proud as a father and provider, and I was happy with my career.

When I look back at my entire experience with Magnum, it is with a big smile on my face and a great sense of accomplishment in my heart.

The oil and gas industry is full of incredible people, with strong work ethics and a formidable tenacity. I cherish the many relationships I've been fortunate enough to keep with the people I've met along the way. I stayed on with Nine Energy Service for approximately eighteen months after the sale, and then I decided to move on to the next chapter in my life. This decision took several months to develop and was very difficult, but I knew in my heart it was time.

When I announced my resignation, I was emotionally overwhelmed by the phone calls, text messages, and emails that my teammates, customers, vendors, and friends sent me. Each of them expressed their best wishes and their gratitude for the opportunity to work at/with a company like Magnum. My sales team even created a video in which several of the women and men whom I'd had the pleasure of managing told stories of how they would not be where they are today without my encouragement, motivation, and leadership. This gesture meant everything to me. It was extremely humbling, and, from time to time, I'll rewatch this video and reminisce about how those relationships signified the best times of my career. In my resignation speech, I saluted them as "the most talented, dedicated, and focused professionals I've ever known." I expressed that I was beyond grateful and honored to have worked with them. I'm confident and content knowing that this experience will likely be the apex of my professional career.

I departed from the oil and gas industry with a plan to take some time off to travel and chase some new experiences with my wife and children. I am pursuing some passion projects I've had in the works for the last few years. One of those is my partnership in Anetik Performance, a global hot weather technical gear company based in San Clemente, California. Anetik's purpose aligns with my values and love for travel, adventure, marketing, product development, fishing, surfing, and other outdoor activities. And those products are the only ones I use while escaping out onto the waters of the Gulf of Mexico. For me, there's something about leaving the safety of land and venturing out on the seas that quenches my thirst for adventure and keeps my spirit alive.

Although it may seem like our three paths are heading in different directions, it's important to me that we keep our common bond intact. I still plan to work with Dad and Derrick on our various investments and projects, as well as opportunities to give back to our community through the Frazier Family Foundation. These projects are a way to stay connected and continue to create and develop ideas together. We are currently in the final stages of renovating a beautiful three-story art deco building in downtown Corpus Christi that will be the headquarters for the Frazier Family office, where we will come together to plan and pursue all our future passion projects and endeavors.

Since I'm an opportunist at heart, the way I look at the future, the possibilities are endless. I'm ready for new challenges, driven by a desire to find my God-given purpose and become my best self while loving and supporting those dearest to me.

CHAPTER 10

TAPPING YOUR FULL POTIENTIAL

Kacy Railsback, my cousin Janet's daughter, a compassionate teacher in a neighboring city, requested that I share my story with her students. Kacy, much like her mother, was incredibly supportive and cared deeply about those around her. In this scenario, Kacy was passionate about these kids and their future. I did not want to let Kacy nor the kids down. I had shared lots of my favorite stories about my life, success, and my business—the age-appropriate stories, anyway. I had just finished giving my talk to a group of middle school students, and I was hoping that what I had shared with them about my path of success in business and in life might have inspired some of them, at least a little bit. If I had planted a seed for somebody, a boy or girl, who would follow his or her own dreams and aspire to really make something of life, I would have felt the visit was well worth my time and energy. I made sure to highlight a few important lessons: Never assume that anybody is smarter than you. Your success will be determined by your own motivation. Look where I started from, I reminded them.

- Even if your parents are struggling in their work or career, or have wound up on welfare, you can still break through barriers and follow your dreams to achieve something big and fulfilling in your life.

- Be sure to shake as many hands as you can because you never know who might turn out to be somebody who can help you along the path to success.

The kids seemed interested in what I had to say, but you never know what's really going to stick. After I finished, a couple of students approached me at the podium as I was packing up my papers to ask me a question. In the middle of speaking to one boy for a couple of minutes, I happened to glance up. While I wasn't watching, the entire class had lined up to greet me, and as they each took their place at the head of the line, they all had the same request: "Could I please shake your hand, Mr. Frazier?"

They had taken to heart what I had said about shaking as many hands as possible, and they were making it a point to start with me! It still gives me goose bumps to remember that moment.

After shaking hands with me, these kids walked away a little more determined to be friendly to everyone already around them in their daily lives and to greet new people they came across, both kids and adults, with a warm hello and a sincere interest. Yep, they had taken a very big step toward success.

Before I left, I made sure to arrange for every kid who came up to me to receive a free ticket to ride the Ferris wheel on North Beach. I told them this was their reward for putting this lesson into action. Of course, I would have given them the passes anyway.

I left school that day more excited about the possibility of reaching young people with my message about succeeding in life. I would especially welcome the chance to speak to college students to share what I learned about pursuing a rewarding and satisfying career.

It would be a pleasure to tell young adults who would soon enter the job market about how I got started. I would have fun telling them about that wildlife refuge starting position that I was all set to take fresh out of college, until I shook an old friend's hand and was pointed toward a job that paid twice as much while opening the door to my entire future. I could emphasize some of the other ideas that helped propel me to heights I had never imagined possible, ideas that we have been shedding light on in this book. These ideas for success include the following:

- **Don't stay stuck in one lane.**

When you look around at what's been happening in the workplace over the last generation or two, it's very clear that this message is more timely and important than ever. Back in the days of our parents or grandparents, it was much more typical to train in one area and then work in that field for most or all of your career, often staying with the same company for twenty-five or thirty years, or longer. How often does that happen today?

You've got to be ready and willing to move this way and that way, following your own interests and pursuing those opportunities that show up on your path at any point along the way. I've known many people who were working in one area for several years, but then they got fired or their company went out of business and boom! They were faced with the need to take a turn, to shift lanes, and they wound up doing something much more interesting and rewarding. If you understand the importance of not getting stuck in one lane, you're better able to make the adjustment and turn that new direction into something that really excites you, something that feeds your hopes, dreams, and ambitions.

Even if you do spend years or even decades in one industry or the same company—whether you own the company or work in support of someone who does—you still need to practice the ability to change lanes when necessary. At Magnum, we claimed our place in oil and gas and rose to higher and higher levels of success by essentially feeding off three major product lines that served oilfield operations: the explosives business, the ceramic disk business, and the composite plug business. But golly, I would hate to think where we would have wound up if we had not been flexible enough to create dozens and dozens of variations or derivatives of those primary products.

We gained a reputation among our customers for our ability and our willingness to think outside the box, to listen to what the customer really needed, and then deliver something new that better met their needs. We had to realize that developing and marketing products and services in our industry was never going to look like the old days of Ford cranking out the same Model A or Model T cars off the assembly line, day after day and year after year. We could not and would not be pigeonholed.

- **Be patient in waiting to discover what flips your trigger, and then follow that path with passion and persistence.**

Sometimes young adults get caught up in the pressure to figure out exactly what they're going to do from early in their college years, or even while still in high school. Then they figure they have to stick with that plan, no matter what. That approach might work for some people, but for others, the real aha moment—the recognition of what they are really meant to do and will pursue with every ounce of their effort and energy—may not come along until sometime much later. And it may arrive at an unexpected time, in an unpredictable way.

In my situation, I was led into the oil industry because I saw an opportunity to make decent money out of college, even though the work had nothing to do with what I had been studying in school. Then, it was a few more years until my trigger really got flipped when I discovered I had a natural design ability and that I could start my own business designing and selling tools and products in the oil industry by listening to my customer's needs.

After that moment of ignition, I was propelled to follow my passions and abilities for thirty-three years of achievement and satisfaction. That could not have happened if I hadn't been receptive to the signs pointing me where I was really meant to go, or if I hadn't had the insight and conviction to say yes to that call.

Today, in the short period of time since we sold Magnum, Garrett and Derrick also have been facing a second round of waiting and listening for what may flip their triggers and send them off to potential new heights.

When I say wait for the trigger to flip, I don't mean sit around at home doing nothing until the spark magically drifts through the window and lands on your shoulder. No way. You do what you need to do to make a solid income and support yourself, utilizing your particular interests and abilities. But at the same time, you listen for that small voice that may someday tell you, "Look, over there—that's what you're meant to be doing!"

- **Make your customer a hero.**

You've heard me mention this guiding force many times to describe our approach at Magnum in attracting and growing business with our clients on all levels of the oil and gas industry. Our aim was to find out exactly what they needed to make their operations go more smoothly, while increasing efficacy and safety and saving them money. This was the goal that shaped the design and development of all our products and equipment, and we were really good at it. That's how we built a business that sold for nearly half a billion dollars.

But this success idea is definitely not limited to the world of oil and gas. If I had wound up running another business, in an entirely different industry, I would have followed the same philosophy in trying to achieve my goals. It's just one of those ideas that translates into any line of work, really. No matter what you do, it's very likely you will have a customer in work or in life, somebody or some entity that you are serving, and your success will depend on how well you perform in a way that makes that customer look and feel like a hero.

Take the time to understand the needs of your own customers, or people you care about. Shape your products or services or whatever you offer in a way that will meet their needs and do so in a way that leaves a satisfied smile on their face. Make yourself and what you offer indispensable.

- **Find your own inspirational sayings and keep coming back to them whenever you need a boost.**

You've heard me talk a lot about that verse that I call "The Uncommon Man," which is often referred to as "An American's Creed." It's amazing how relevant the words of that verse are to me even today. I'll share that verse again here:

I DO NOT CHOOSE TO BE A COMMON MAN.

It is my right to be uncommon—if I can. I seek opportunity— not security. I do not wish to be a kept citizen, humbled and dulled by having a company look after me.

I want to take the calculated risk; to dream and to build, to fail and to succeed.

I refuse to barter incentive for a dole. I prefer the challenges of life to the guaranteed existence; the thrill of fulfillment to the stale calm of utopia.

> **It is my heritage to stand erect, proud, and unafraid;**
> **to think and act for myself, enjoy the benefits of my creations,**
> **and to face the world boldly and say, this I have done.**

I can go through almost line by line and relate Dean Alfange's words directly to my beliefs and my experience in building our business. Here are a few examples:

I seek opportunity—not security.

When I launched Magnum on the basis of developing one new product that I designed, I sure didn't have absolute security that I could sustain and grow a highly profitable business. I had a dream and a belief in myself and what I was trying to do. I just took that opportunity that I had been seeking and squeezed it with all the strength I had.

That way of approaching business just fit for me because I'm an eternal optimist. I will always look for the upside of an opportunity rather than the downside, whether that opportunity relates to a business, a house, a piece of land, a development project, or a vehicle. I just welcome the opportunity and say to myself, "Oh, I could do this."

I want to take the calculated risk; to dream and to build, to fail and to succeed.

Although I never want to be held back by a need for security, I certainly don't go out of my way looking to take crazy risks. On a trip to Vegas once, I entered a casino allowing myself to spend up to $2,000. But when I sat down at the blackjack table and lost ten bucks on my first hand, I immediately said, "Nah, I'm not staying here. I'm done." I'm not much of a risk taker when it comes to something with really lousy odds of success.

When I do take the calculated risk, as I did in launching Magnum in 1985, I am driven by that desire to dream and to build. I was absolutely confident that if I could achieve a little success at one stage of running my business, I could build on that success and keep on going forward. And I could do that again and again and again. On my march forward, I knew that

I would have situations where I would fail at something I tried and briefly stumble backward. But as most entrepreneurs will tell you, failure is an inherent part of achieving success. If you get knocked down, you just keep getting back and going a little bit further, and a little bit further beyond that.

I prefer the challenges of life to the guaranteed existence . . .

Everywhere in life, not just in operating a business, I like to experience different challenges. I've always enjoyed going to new places, even when some of those new places presented some pretty big challenges! I like to try new things in life. Learning AutoCAD was one of many examples. I don't believe in stepping too far out, but far enough to keep life exciting. If you don't take any chances, you'll never even cross the road to find out what's on the other side.

The thrill of fulfillment to the stale calm of utopia.

As a kid, I enjoyed the excitement of jumping off that barge canal bridge with my friends. It was a thrilling act, and when you landed safely you certainly felt a sense of fulfillment. But I'll admit, if that bridge had been ten feet higher, I probably would have held back. I like going for something that will give me a thrill but won't kill me!

With Magnum, we were definitely experiencing the thrill of fulfillment and steering away from any stale calm of utopia, when we kept rejecting all those offers to sell the company before finally accepting the big proposal from Nine Energy Service. When each new offer was placed on the table in front of us, I would turn to Garrett and Derrick and say, "Guys, look at the profits we're turning now. We can keep moving this thing forward. We can double our size again and again!" That was much more of a thrill than if I had said, "Well, we've made some money here. Let's just cash in and go home."

Tapping Your Full Potential

It is my heritage to stand erect, proud, and unafraid . . .

Those words send me back to my experience of earning a spot on the Texas A&I–Kingsville football team as a walk-on, and then fighting and scratching my way to earning a full scholarship. Physically, I was one of the smallest guys on that team. And in stature, the other guys came in with reputations as superstars and all-state honors. But right from the first scrimmage, I was not afraid to go in there and play with an attitude that screamed, "Hey, I belong here!" I stood erect and proud, and I reaped the dividends.

To think and act for myself . . .

When I first learned how to use AutoCAD and began creating my own designs for tools and products in oil and gas, I didn't care what other people and other businesses were doing. I was determined to find my own way of designing tools that would be simpler and more effective than what others were developing and selling. Over the years, I probably designed thousands of tools, and I didn't copy any of them. I wanted that feeling of being able to come up with something and then show it to a customer and say, "I did that."

Enjoy the benefits of my creations . . .

I always enjoyed the satisfaction of seeing what I had created become a successful part of our operation, helping us to grow and prosper. Then, as the business became more successful, and finally when we sold our company, I was finding more and more ways to simply enjoy and appreciate not only the monetary benefits but also the new and exciting doors that opened up for me.

To face the world boldly and say, this I have done.

Those words call to mind my growing desire to leave a legacy, to create something that has my name on it and that I can be proud of. Most of my family and friends and others I have met know something about what I have built and how hard I have worked to achieve our success. They could nod and smile with me as I sold Magnum and said, "This I have done." Now, with the new projects and developments I am pursuing, I welcome the opportunity to have others see something with my name on it and know that Lynn Frazier helped to make it happen.

When you think about all these success ideas, is there some common thread that ties them all together? I think maybe there is. When you follow these guiding principles, or any other phrases that will help motivate and inspire you, what you're really doing is seeking to tap your full potential in your profession and your life.

I've always felt strongly that we all have the ability to actualize our true potential. And as I tell young people today, you should never underestimate what that potential is in you.

In other words, don't be afraid to aspire to do or be something that people around you try to tell you is too big or too far outside the box they see you in. Strive to reach that full potential that you recognize in yourself.

When I go around my community or spend time getting to know people in places where I travel, I always see so much potential in individuals of any age or life situation. I sometimes find myself saying to myself, "Oh, if you just did THIS or stopped doing THAT, the sky would be the limit for what you could do." But I know that ultimately, it's that person's choice of what they will or will not aspire to or try to make happen.

I also believe that our towns, our cities, and our country have their own version of potential, and I'm just as interested in those places realizing their full potential too. That's part of my motivation behind my investment in development projects in Corpus Christi.

When it comes to our individual path of trying to tap our full potential, if I had to point to one major approach that can strengthen anyone's chances of becoming the best version of themselves in work and in life, it would be this idea expressed by Albert Einstein:

*"Stay away from negative people.
They have a problem for every solution."*

To me, that's it in a nutshell. Don't be negative, be positive. Don't see the problem, see the solution. When you look at a challenging situation, the first words out of your mouth should not be something that points out the problems: "Golly, look at this, look at that. It's never going to work." If you look at your life and the situations you encounter in that negative way, what do you suppose is going to happen? You probably won't achieve your potential in life.

Instead, consider the change if the first words out of your mouth sounded something like this: "What if somebody did this or did that? Wouldn't that work?" That's how you find a solution for every problem that you face, rather than pointing to some possible problem. When you follow this positive approach, you can aspire to be the best you can be. You can strive to be the best there is in whatever you're doing.

For myself, I didn't really know when I launched Magnum that I would compete with the largest companies in the world, or that these big companies would be buying my products. But that didn't deter me from striving to make that happen. I kept taking baby steps forward, and with each of those small steps I focused on finding a solution, not getting bogged down by the size and scope of the problem. And I found myself saying, "Wow, now I'm selling to these guys; maybe tomorrow I can start selling to THOSE guys too!" That's how our full potential as a business was actualized. Even now, I'm keeping my eyes open for new ways to reach my potential: really slowing down so I can be more available for those I love and finding new opportunities to show my fun-loving, relaxed way of being.

Tapping your full potential is not necessarily about achieving some specific financial goal or attaining a certain status. The way I look at it, the more we are able to reach our potential, the better our life will be. When we strive to reach our potential, and we see and feel the progress that we're making on our path, we're just going to enjoy ourselves a whole lot more than if we don't make this commitment.

If things are coming together for you because of your efforts to tap your potential, you're more apt to start walking around with a smile. You'll be happier. And isn't that a lot of what life is about, being happy?

We all want the chance to do those things that make us happy, things that we enjoy, things that make life truly worth living. We want to have fun, and we want to feel satisfied. It's just innate in us as humans. And we all have our own favorite ways of being really happy.

For me, that includes finding more time to be with those I love, to do things for others I care about. I'm also happy when I'm riding in my boat. And I'm always happy whenever I can just relax, enjoy my favorite beverages, and soak up the environment in one of my favorite beach areas.

As I've mentioned, the Caymans really flips my switch. The warm weather, the gentle waves, the natural beauty, and the pristine condition they keep everything in just create a winning combination. It's no coincidence that I displayed a large mural of a Caymans beach scene on the wall of one of my offices. It just fits the bill for my favorite kind of ocean environment.

If I had to put together the perfect fantasy beach scene that would always make me happy, it would include calm water, a long stretch of white-sand beach (the whiter the better!), lots of well-maintained palm trees, a couple of chairs for friends or loved ones, pristine grounds, and buildings nearby. My favorite alcoholic drinks would be at my fingertips, along with chips and dip, and maybe some local fish. I would be wearing shorts or swim trunks with one of my favorite Hawaiian shirts. And, of course, the scene would not be complete without the soft sounds of my favorite kind of music, which happens to be what I call beach country music: Jimmy Buffett, Luke Bryan, Kenny Chesney, and singers like that.

It helps to be on an island, although I don't need my own private "Frazier Island." I'm too social for that. But it needs to be in an area that's developed in a sophisticated manner. If you have a house or a restaurant with a thatched roof to capture the look and feel of the local area, it should look nice, organized, and be well kept up. This helps minimize any stress for me.

This beach scene makes me happy in many different ways. It's not just the relaxing and beautiful scene. For me, and for most people I know, there's just something about the sound of the calm waves coming off the ocean that's so soothing and relaxing to your system. It puts me in a more peaceful and relaxed state so that when I leave my happy beach scene, I can go on and do what I need and want to do to continue to strive for something new, for something more.

So, that's a quick description of some of what makes me happy. What is it for you? What really makes you feel content? What brings you the greatest sense of joy? What allows you to sink into a deeply peaceful state?

And what steps can you take in your life today to strive toward reaching your full potential so that you can bring more and more of what makes you happy into your life every day?

ACKNOWLEDGMENTS

There are many people who have been important and encouraging on the road to writing this book. At great risk of leaving someone out, we wish to acknowledge:

- Family and Friends
  - Mom and Dad, for their work ethic, respect and high regard for others. Their zest for life of adventure and ambition is something that has always stuck with me.
  - To my brothers and sister: Lloyd for being an inspiration as a mechanical genius; Michelle, the artist, singer and engineer; and Lorne, the little brother I always watched out for, his positivity and readiness for the next adventure.
  - Trish Frazier, my second wife, best friend, sounding board, confidant, and right-and-left-hand person while I was running the roads, world traveling, designing, and building Magnum.

- She was all things administrative as well as uber organized which was a very crucial aspect to helping me build Magnum.
  - Mike Maryan, one of my best friends, your dynamic personality, positivity, and infectious attitude which I always want to be around. I never let you far out of my sight.
  - Cynthia Frazier, my high school sweetheart and the mother of my two sons. Early on she put her teaching career on hold to help me start and run a sporting goods and t-shirt printing business. After that chapter, she continued to run the business and I transitioned into going out on my own in oil and gas with confidence, which allowed me to chase my aspirations. Her perseverance and commitment to do whatever it takes to make her customer happy was an inspiration to me. She's thoughtful, cares for others more than herself, and she puts her family first above all.
- Don McAda at Vann Tool Company
  - To my first boss, for continually inspiring me to be the best individual I could be. You believed in me and brought the best out of me. I never wanted to let you down and I hope I never did. Your vision was unbridled and inspiring.
- Norm and Angela Lussier and their son Michael who owned Prime Perforating in Calgary, CAN, who employed me as a sales, operations, and design consultant of a new division of their company. You had the drive to build a business with character from top to bottom. Your hospitality will forever inspire me.
  - Magnum PI
  - Jim McDaniel, my first introduction to an individual who embodied the spirit of the oilfield. Jim showed me the ropes of

wireline operations. His extensive knowledge allowed me to cut my teeth . . .

- Magnum TCP
  - Dar Torres
    - My first employee and partner. Thank you for believing in me and my crazy dream to step out on our own, and for your contributions in introducing me to mid-continent oil and gas network and creating our customer base.
  - Drake Andarakes
    - Your larger-than-life persona inspired me. I knew that if I were to ever be half the salesman you are, I had some big shoes to fill. At 6'5, your charisma and drive established our base in Oklahoma, the surrounding areas, and the rest of world.
  - Thad Sperry
    - Your mechanical mindset was a foundation for our success. Your structure for our Operations allowed us to move forward with confidence. Thank you for collaborating with me to make our systems efficient and effective.
- Magnum Oil Tools
  - Ron Abt, and your beautiful wife, Yelena. Your approach to work and life was instrumental to our success. Your support and structure allowed me to focus and dream up the next product. Your 6Ps laid the tracks for the rest of the team.
  - Bob Scott, your network and connections in the Canadian oil patch and your commitment to drive any distance just to see your customers face to face across Canada was the springboard

for our Northern success. Your unrelenting work ethic and reliability created the confidence we needed.

- Ken Yong, my creative counterpart, the Yin to my Yang. Your intuition, common sense, vision, and knack for making things work made our design process effortless and fun.

- Brandon Munòz, for taking a chance to move down to Corpus to be with your mom, our family, and be a part of Magnum. Thank you for your dedication to meeting the company's goals and improving our inside sales processes. You helped Magnum gain significant market share when you found your strength in West Texas sales.

- Leah Schexnayder, our financial main sail, your dedication and knowledge to all things financial are invaluable and second to none. Your relentless drive and caring heart were the foundation for our worldwide family business.

- Lisa Papenfuss, your growth from a young girl to an incredibly successful businesswoman was inspiring to be a part of. Thank you for jumping in, grabbing the bull by the horns, and growing alongside us. It has been a pleasure to watch you grow your beautiful family while playing a valuable role at Magnum.

- Janice Shanks, a mother to us all, keeping us and accounts payable in line. Thank you for your hard work, inspiring others, and contributions to our culture.

- Keller Harvey, with a heart the size of Texas, his unbridled support and dedication to our success was second to none. He took on any task that was thrown his way with conviction and complementary vision to our goals.

- Kevin Branch, our ghost writer, thank you for your patience and ability to pull stories deeply hidden in our memory banks. You have constructed an inspiring narrative from our wild ride.

Acknowledgments

- To the forward-thinking leaders at Magnum Oil Tools who carried the responsibility of doing the work to make our customers heroes across the world.

Abrego, Justin Jeffrey
Abt, Ronald
Acaster, Lynn
Alarcon, Humberto V
Aleman, Reynaldo
Amaro, Jamon
Amos, Christy
Amundson, Jeffrey A
Angeles, Joel L
Antonetz, Nathan
Arbuckle, Sean
Arfsten, Jeremy
Arias, Andrew
Arredondo, Tracey
Atkins, Taylor
Atkinson, Darren
Atkinson, Whitney
Bailey, Steven
Bain, Tammy
Barrera II, Roberto
Barrera III, Roberto
Beauregard, Grayson
Beck, William
Bedford, William
Beltran, John
Benavides, Elizabeth B
Benavidez, Jason
Bennetsen, Justin
Bennett, Kalea
Bennett, Stephanie D
Benton, Brandon
Berg, Brian
Blair, Rose
Bohn, Heather
Bolding, Wesley
Borden, John
Brandt, Justin
Briseno, Guadalupe Omar
Brittain, Scott
Brittain, Stephen
Buendel, Tiffany
Buhidar, Brett
Burns, Joe D
Bush Jr, Kenneth
Cano Jr, Javier
Cano, Javier
Cantu, Christopher
Cantu, James P
Cardenas, Richard
Carlisle, Taylor
Carnes, Jacob
Carpenter, Michael
Carver, Christopher
Carver, Victor
Casarez, Adan
Casey, Bryan
Casey, Bryan J
Casey, Cari
Castrejon, Bobby
Castro, Shea
Cavazos, Laura L
Champion, Krystle L
Chaudoir, Joseph
Chaudoir, Magdalena
Chaudoir, Mark
Chavira, Yasmin
Choi, William
Clary, Sammy
Cleveland, Travis
Coleman, Carri L
Cordero, Joel V
Cortez, Moses
Curiel, Lydia
Curry, Valeria
Curtis, Danny
Davila Jr, Jose
Davila, Ashley Brittany
Davila, Jose
Davis, Douglas L
Deanda, Faith
Deis, Scott
Delaune, Darryl
Dennis, Dan S
Downey, John
Duckett, Eric
Dudley, Coleman K
Duncan, Jackson K
Duncan, Scott
Easter, Jenilee
Edmondson, Cordarius J
Elliot, Shawn
Evans, Christopher
Ewers, Phillip

Farber, Scott	Goree, Katy Marie	Johnson, Erica
Favela, Michael	Granger, Gerald G	Kaderka, Brandon
Figueiredo, Johana	Groce, Rachel	Kelley, Alvin B
Fiscus, Bryan	Guerra, Isidro	Kennedy, Edward
Flemming, Ray	Guerra, Rolando	Kenyon, Michael P
Foster, Jeremiah	Guerrero, Albert J	Kinnamon, Mallory
Franco, Valarie R	Guillen, Juan	Krouse, Jerret
Freeman, Marcos	Gunter, Jarrett	Kuhn, Brian
Frye, Andrew R	Gutierrez, Araceli	Laue, Marc
Gangstad, Erik	Gutierrez, Gabriel	Lawrence, Keith A
Garcia III, Jesus	Gutierrez, Michael	Leal, Edward
Garcia Jr, Francisco	Gutierrez, Miguel A	Leal, Matthew Gregory
Garcia-Brooks, Debra	Gutierrez, Robert	Lewis, Nathaniel
Garcia, Adrian	Guzman, Arturo	Lieber, Michael
Garcia, Amador	Haley, Jody Dean	Lindsey, Jamey
Garcia, Gina G	Hanke, Thomas J	Long, David
Garcia, Isaac R	Harness, Steven	Longoria, Justin
Garcia, Jesus	Harvey, Keller	Lopez, Jose
Garcia, Kayla	Hatley, Ashton	Lujan, Harrison
Garcia, Mary E.	Haugen, Dylan	Luna, Jaythan M
Garcia, Samuel	Hayes, Landon	Maccoul, David
Garfield, Garry	Hedrick, Robbie	Maldonado, Matthew
Garza, Deborah	Hernandez, Alberto	Manning, Chad
Garza, Lisa	Hernandez, Alejandro	Manuel, Michele
Gentry, Dustin	Hernandez, Carmen	Marquez II, Mark
Gerdes, Justin R	Hernandez, Jason	Martinez Jr, Aniceto
Gilge, Rodger	Hernandez, Jimmy	Martinez, Aniceto
Glasgow, Roger D	Hernandez, Mario	Martinez, Arlene
Gomez, Domynick	Hernandez, Rosendo	Martinez, Eduardo
Gomez, Nicholas	Hilton, Lynae	Martinez, Eric
Gonzales, Alexander	Hogan, Stephanie L	Martinez, Frank
Gonzales, Timothy	Holte, Darwin	Martinez, Juan
Gonzalez, Cristel M	Hooper, Steven A	Martinez, Pablo
Gonzalez, Emily	Howard, Jacqueline D	Maryan, Philip
Gonzalez, Jairo	Ince, Christen	Mata, Jr, Jose
Gonzalez, Lillian	Jedkins, Robyn	Maya, Jason

Acknowledgments

Maya, Jose Miguel
Maya, Juan
Mayhair, Nicholas B
Mazurek, Jeffry
McCabe, Laura Elizabeth
McCabe, Victoria
McCain, Joanna
McCann, Cameron
McCauley, Andrew
McClain, Johnathan
McDaniel, Terrence
McDonagh, Mark
McElwee, Lester J
McKenzie, Christopher
McKinnis, Wesley Ryan
McMullin, Derek W
McNair, Joshua
McQueen, Chad
Medrano, Israel
Medrano, Robert
Medrano, Sylvia
Meisner, Brent
Melman, Benjamin
Mendez, Armando
Mendez, Denise
Mendietta, Jose Orlando
Mendoza, Blanca E
Mernaugh, Nicholas
Mernaugh, Ryan
Metcalf, Lee
Meza Chavira, Sandra A
Miller, Alex
Milton, Benjamin
Mingboupha, Mitch
Mook, Andrew
Moore, Christina

Moore, Schuyler
Morales, Jose
Moreno, Alcaria
Moreno, Julian
Moses, Trenton B
Mosley, Mark
Munoz, Brandon
Murdoch, Julie
Narvaez, Anthony
Navarro, John
Newberry, Jon-Marc C
Nichols, Rusty W
Nobles-Dubose, Ashley
Norwood, Mary
Novosad, Benjamin
Noyola, Tomas
Nyberg, Ryan T
O'Neill, Jenny
Obregon, Desiree
Olguin, Francisco
Olvera Jr, Guillermo
Ortiz, Rolando
Pace, Chance
Pacsi, Brittany Rae
Papenfuss, Andrew
Papenfuss, Lisa
Park, Wonjoon
Parks, Jeffrey W
Parry, Chase R
Pate, Justin
Paulson, James Paul
Perales, Melquiades
Perez, Jared
Perez, Rebecca
Perez, Ricardo
Perez, Venessa

Perkins, James
Perrigue, Krystal M
Petersen, Stephanie
Peterson, Keith
Phillips, James G
Pinder, Andrew
Potter, Karl Matthew
Prado, Lauren
Prado, Melissa
Rabel, Milton J
Ramirez, Amy
Ramirez, Christina
Ramos, Julie L
Rasco, Robert
Recio, Amber L
Reeves, Brian
Reeves, James
Reeves, Roland
Reiley, Joshua
Reyes, Anthony A
Reyes, Elias R
Reyes, Israel
Reyna, Enrique
Rheam, Zacharia D
Richards, Thomas E
Riley, Sara
Rivas, Abraham
Roberts, Coby
Roche, Timothy M
Rodriguez, Adan
Rodriguez, Angel
Rodriguez, Deciderio
Rodriguez, Emmanuel
Rodriguez, Frank
Rodriguez, Juan
Rodriguez, Ruby R

Romero, Eddie
Rouse, Robert
Rowland, Holly M
Salaiz, Rodolfo
Salazar, Jesus
Salinas, Jesse
Sanchez, Daniel
Sanchez, Juan
Sanchez, Marissa
Sanchez, Steven
Sanders, Sarah
Saneel, Mohsen
Schexnayder, Leah
Schiro, Lee
Schiro, Morgan
Scott, Robert (Bob)
Shanks, Eric
Shanks, Janice
Shepherd, Norma J
Silva, Michael
Silva, Scott
Simon, Aaron
Simpson, Joshua
Smolik, Judith H
Smoot, Alma J

Smoot, Jake A
Snyder, Melissa I
Snyder, Valeria
Solis, Gabriel
Solis, Ignacio A
Sones, Andrew
Squire, Jennifer A
Steele, Michael
Stimson, Bianca
Streiff, Jason B
Stubbs, Cory J
Stubbs, John C
Suarez, Sammy
Swainston, Keith S
Tave, Elizabeth
Tavera, Juan
Thiel, Jaydin
Thompson, Landon J
Tijerina, Maximo
Tomscha, Jeremy
Torres, Marcus
Tringali, Cameron
Valdez, Misty
Valdez, Ricardo
Valdez, Robert

Valencia, Michael
Vargas, Michael
Vasquez III, Mario
Vasquez, Amanda
Vasquez, Ryan
Vazquez, Erik
Vega, Raul
Villa, Patricia R
Villalobos, Jose
Villanueva, Veronica
Villarreal, Valarie
Vines, Donald R
Wallace, Melissa
Warrenfeltz, Larry Todd
Weiss, Connie
White, Billy
Winkler, James M
Winn, Cory D
Yanez, Christina
Ybarra, Irene
Ybarra, Patrick J
Yong, Lakhena (Ken)
Zeinert, Richard C

www.ingramcontent.com/pod-product-compliance
Lightning Source LLC
Chambersburg PA
CBHW030521080526
44586CB00011B/285